THE COLOR TREASURY OF

EIGHTEENTH CENTURY PORCELAIN

Fig. 1. Vase, China, K'ang-Hsi Period, around 1700

THE COLOR TREASURY OF

Eighteenth Century PORCELAIN

Text by SIEGFRIED DUCRET
Photographs by MICHAEL WOLGENSINGER
Translated by CHRISTINE FRIEDLANDER

THOMAS Y. CROWELL COMPANY
Established 1834 New York

My sincere thanks to all those who assisted me with illustrations:
Frau Dr. H. Meyer
Dr. Pauls
Prof. Dr. E. Schneider
Herr Paul Schnyder von Wartensee
Dr. A. Torré
Dr. Weinberg, New York
Dr. A. Wiederkehr

The following museums:
Staatliche Kunstsammlungen, Porzellansammlung, Dresden
Historisches Museum, Frankfurt
Musée d'Art et d'Histoire, Geneva
Victoria and Albert Museum, London
Archiv der Porzellanmanufaktur VEB, Meissen
Württembergisches Landesmuseum, Stuttgart
Museum für angewandte Kunst, Vienna

Designed by Abigail Moseley

PRINTED IN BELGIUM
by OFFSET VAN DEN BOSSCHE

Library of Congress Cataloging in Publication Data

Ducret, Siegfried.
The color treasury of 18th century porcelain.
Includes index.

1. Color in the ceramic industries. 2. Porcelain.
I. Wolgensinger, Michael. II. Title.
NK4373.D7813 1976 738.2'094 76-10734
ISBN 0-690-01124-5

10 9 8 7 6 5 4 3 2 1

CONTENTS

INTRODUCTION

It is impossible to think of the splendid noble courts of Europe in the eighteenth century without being reminded of the history of European porcelain. The absolute monarch of Saxony perceived it his duty to impress the world with magnificent ornamental decorations as symbols of his grandeur.

The word *porcelain* was coined by the Venetian navigator Marco Polo, who served the Mongol Emperor Kublai Khan for seventeen years. In his *Description of the World* of 1298, he described how in the capital of Tingui, porcelain jars of great beauty and delicacy were being fired. The name porcelain, which has survived for centuries, was derived from the Latin word *porcella* (suckling pig). This was also the name for a Mediterranean shell, which during Marco Polo's time was used as currency in China. He compared its color with that of porcelain. No doubt, Marco Polo embellished its manufacture with a vivid imagination. It was only in 1717 that the missionary Father D'Entrecolle discovered that the porcelain of Ching-te-chen was a product of two different types of clay: kaolin, named after the Kaoling Pass where it was found, and Petuntse (feldspar, chalk, quartz, and calcium as flux).

Chinese Porcelain

Chinese porcelain has been greatly admired everywhere and at all times. It is not surprising that porcelain was invented in China. The invention of gunpowder, rag paper, the processes of early printing and woodcut are all linked to the name China. They were the evidence of the inventive spirit of this ancient culture, which also found the formula for the first true porcelain. According to the latest research, this porcelain was fired during the West Chou period, as early as 1300 B.C. Temperatures of 1,000 to 1,300 degrees were needed to fire it. A few porcelain vessels with carved relief ornamentation are preserved from the Tang period (A.D. 618–907). The later dynasties of the Emperors Sung and Ming lavished much attention on these so-called industries. The most highly prized vases were painted in an underglaze cobalt blue. Even after Meissen had rediscovered the technique of reproducing this color, well-executed blue porcelain was regarded as particularly valuable, since it had taken years of laborious experimentation to achieve satisfactory results.

The Chinese vase (Fig. 1) is painted in underglaze blue and may have been produced between 1662 and 1722, during the reign of the Emperor K'ang Hsi, in Ching-te-chen. It was brought to Europe on one of the typical sailing ships (Fig. 2) belonging to one of the many East India Companies.

The first Chinese porcelain arrived in Europe via Venice and Constantinople during the early Middle Ages. After the discovery of the ocean passage around the Cape of Good Hope by Vasco da Gama, Europe entered into a lively trade with China and East Asia. The Portuguese were the first to bring Chinese porcelain to Europe in 1514, and soon all the treasures of the Far East were coming together in Lisbon. The first factory was opened in Canton in 1657. In 1560 the Dutch were already in possession of 800 merchant ships manned by 30,000 sailors. The Spaniards and French were to follow.

In 1612 one sailor brought back 38,641 pieces of porcelain, and another, 69,057 pieces of tableware. In 1734 a Dutch ship carried as many as 300,000 tea cups, 80,000 pair of coffee cups, 2,000 fruit bowls, 1,658 rosewater bottles, and 187 chamber pots. Every East India Company also imported enormous quantities of silk, spices, lacquer ware, tea, fabric, sugar, diamonds, and *magots* (treasures).

It was understandable that all over Europe artisans searched for the mysterious formula that could produce this "miracle porcelain."

Experiments were attempted at the courts of Pesaro, Turin, and Ferrara, but these were insignificant compared to Florence, where Francis Medici I had conducted experiments since the middle of the sixteenth century. It was of course Italy which first won fame. Had it not, as early as the sixteenth century, presented the world with its lovely maiolicas of Orvieto, Urbino, Caffagiola, Deruta, and Faenza? However, Francis was not able to fire true porcelain, but only the soft-paste porcelain, made of frit and painted cobalt blue, in the manner of Chinese porcelain. A few vases, most of them shaped as the faiences of Urbino, are in the larger museums of London, Paris, Florence, and New York.

Fig. 2. Detail of a Meissen painting. Sailing ship of the *Compagnie des Indes*

European porcelain was invented for the first time in Dresden thanks to the generosity of August the Strong, Elector of Saxony and King of Poland—a monarch of quite unusual character. Porcelain is being manufactured in the Albrechtsburg in Meissen to this day (Fig. 3).

"It is one of the most interesting inventions ever made. A veritable triumph of human intelligence. There are few similar examples throughout the history of human inventions that equal this deliberate re-invention of Chinese porcelain." (Zimmermann, 1908, in *Invention and Early Period of Chinese Porcelain.)*

August the Strong

August II was called the Strong, as it was told that he could break a horseshoe in one hand, squash a thaler in the other, and lift a ball weighing 396 pounds (180 kg). The legend tells that he was raised on lion's milk. As an indispensable part of his education, he visited all the noble courts of Europe. According to an eighteenth-century account, "He broke the ladies' hearts as he broke horseshoes. Venice was then the university of worldliness. According to the mandatory rules of Italian chivalry, he spent his days in the churches wooing the daughters of the nobility who lived, outside the church's jurisdiction, in the monasteries of the islands Murano and San Giorgio, as nuns without veil with the title Eccelenza."

In 1694 Friedrich August became Elector of Saxony at the age of twenty-four, and three years later, in 1697, he was King of Poland. However, no Protestant head could wear the royal crown of Poland, which was indeed worth a Mass. On June 2, 1697, in Baden near Vienna, August secretly converted to Catholicism. His change of religion was greeted with exultation in Poland and with shock and grief in the Lutheran Saxony.

The Swedish War under Sweden's King Charles XII cost August the kingdom of Poland and even the Electorate of Saxony was occupied by Sweden. In this situation an alchemist appeared as a gift from heaven. Even if it should take years of experimenta-

Fig. 3. Albrechtsburg in Meissen. Seat of the *Manufaktur Meissen* in the 18th century. Peep-show illustration from the first half of the 18th century

tion, he could not fail to be successful in the end. August never wavered in his belief.

The judgment of posterity is divided on the merits and achievements of this typically baroque monarch. One opinion expressed during the nineteenth century may have been to the point: "His keen intelligence lacked the support of a firm character. His striving for success shunned the sweat of labor. His passions did not know the limits of a sense of duty. His pleasure seeking ignored consideration and manners." These were hard words, but they are mitigated by the legacy he left to posterity, the European porcelain.

J. F. Boettger

At the end of October 1701 there was much excitement in the city of Berlin. An apprentice of the apothecary Zorn in Neumarkt could make gold! He had proved this in the presence of the family Zorn and two clergymen. His name was Johann Friedrich Boettger, and he was nineteen years old. The Greek monk Lascaris had given a tincture to the young apprentice, which enabled him to turn common metals into gold.

Obviously the young alchemist was not feeling too

comfortable in Berlin, for when the King of Prussia began to show interest in his art, Boettger fled the city in the dark of night. A Prussian officer with twelve soldiers was ordered to pursue him and was promised a reward of 1,000 thalers if he could seize the alchemist. Boettger managed to escape across the Elbe to Wittenberg in Saxony. His fame had preceded him. He was safe from the Prussians, but he had jumped out of the frying pan into the fire.

The Saxon court emissary wrote in a letter of November 9 from Wittenberg to Dresden: "We can congratulate ourselves if this alchemist really succeeds in making gold in Saxony, thereby ending its scarcity." The King was in Poland at the time and issued orders to his deputy Egon von Fuerstenberg to take Boettger into custody and bring him from Wittenberg to Dresden, where his activities could be watched.

To make gold had been a serious occupation among the innumerable alchemists since the sixteenth century. Their theory was based on the hypothesis that all matter was composed of three basic elements: mercury, sulphur, and salts. Gold was distinguished from other metals only by a different combination of the three basic substances: "With metals, through metals, metals are formed" (Paracelsus). Even persons of intelligence and learning believed in this transmutation, and one of them was August II.

Fig. 4. Plate of Boettger stoneware marked with the initials AR (Augustus Rex), around 1710

In the meantime, a plot was hatched in Berlin to abduct Boettger from Dresden. The plan was discovered, and Boettger was taken to the castle where a laboratory equipped with all the needed utensils and tools was put at his disposal. The famous physicist and mathematician Ehrenfried Walther von Tschirnhaus (1655–1708) of Kieslingswalde in the Lausitz district was engaged as scientific assistant.

Tschirnhaus, a man of the world in touch with the scientific community, had presented Saxony with a grinding and polishing mill for precious stones, a glass industry, and a factory for blue dye. While staying with his friend Homberg in Paris in 1701, he erroneously believed that he had discovered the secret formula for Chinese porcelain. Boettger knew about these experiments, and he also was well aware that his own experiments with various dyes would not be crowned by success. He escaped to Vienna on June 20, 1703 but was apprehended and brought back. The King was unshaken in his belief that his alchemist would find the mysterious tincture within a short time. In 1705 Boettger was taken to the Albrechtsburg, where Papst, the Freiberger Councilor of Mines, and twelve foundry workers, including Wildenstein, Koehler, Stoelzel, and the court physician Dr. Bartelmei, were to assist him. Twenty-four furnaces were put at his disposal.

Fruitless experiments were conducted up to September 5, 1706. That day Boettger was brought to the fortress Koenigstein to protect him from the approaching Swedish army. Arrangements were made for "Sir Notus with three servants" to be provided with anything he might need, and only after the end of hostilities was he returned to his laboratory on the Venusbastei in Dresden. He had by now squandered 40,000 thalers without any success at all.

At this point the scientist Tschirnhaus intervened. With the help of enormous burning glasses, he had melted tin, copper, and brass, and also bricks, chalk,

Fig. 5. Small tea pot. Boettger stoneware with relief decoration of branches and *almandines* (set in rubies). Decorated by Johann Friedrich Meyer, around 1710

and other materials. Since Boettger knew only too well that, as with other alchemists, the noose was tightening around his neck, he allied himself closely with Tschirnhaus. Together they examined the colored clays which previously had played an important role in alchemy. Under the supervision of Michael Nemitz, Tschirnhaus solved the technical problems, while Dr. Bartelmei worked on the composition of the paste. A decree issued by August the Strong in November 1707 declared that it was Boettger's duty to save a destitute Saxony by the establishment of porcelain factories.

Boettger's first actual attempt to produce porcelain took place in November 1707. He succeeded in producing red stoneware on the Venusbastei in Dresden. Because of the immense heat of his furnaces, his laboratory would have been destroyed by fire on New Year's night, 1707–1708, had it not been for the intervention of the fire brigade. His staff now consisted of twenty persons and cost the Elector 382 thalers a month. He was aware of the irony of his situation when he composed a little rhyme stating that "the great creator God had made a potter of an alchemist."

By December 1707, the King was quite pleased with his impostor alchemist. When he saw that the ceramic experiments were progressing, he raised the available funds to 530 thalers and later to 750 thalers.

The first red stoneware fired at high temperatures consisted of iron rich bolus from Nuremberg and soluble clay from the soil at Plaue. Later on Boettger used red clay from Zwickau. The stoneware could be polished and cut. Even the brick factory of a Herr Ruehle in Dresden-Neustadt was working on its production. The workers labored from five o'clock in the morning to seven o'clock in the evening with three rest periods.

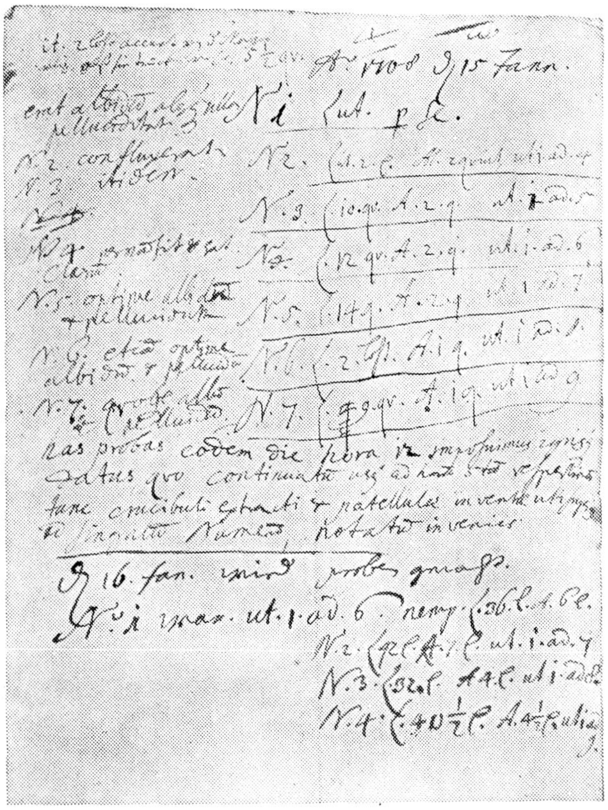

Boettger fired a dinner service for the King, carving the initials AR (Augustus Rex) in each plate (Fig. 4). Johann David Kratzberg was a particularly able artist and was ordered to produce speedily fifty large vases "whereby he is to take care that they be equal to one another." A few small stoneware pitchers produced by Boettger still exist. They are decorated with relief ornaments of flowering sprigs and are painted with multicolor enamel paint. "These delicate paintings are strikingly alive," wrote the director of the large Meissen porcelain collection in Dresden, Frau Menzhausen, and not without justification. The effect is emphasized by small inlaid rubies (Fig. 5). The artist who decorated Saxon glass in the same manner was Johann Friedrich Meyer. He was enamellist at the court of Saxony from 1710 to 1720. As he was not named among the members of the *Manufakturverwandten* (members of the manufacturing family), as they were called then, he must have been commissioned by Boettger.

Boettger also invented a deep black glaze of manganese and cobalt, which was decorated with enamel colors and gold (Fig. 6). The vessels were formed by the potter Peter Eggebrecht from Delft; the relief decorations were modeled by the sculptor Bernard Miller. After 1711 Miller was replaced by the goldsmith Johann-Jacob Irminger, who also was teaching the potters and modelers in the Albrechtsburg. The models were made of wood, and these wood models were used to make the plaster molds. Chinese and Dutch vases were copied frequently. In 1710 Boettger sent stoneware worth 3,857 thalers to the Easter Fair at Leipzig for the first time.

But the red stoneware was not porcelain! The factory archives in Meissen have in their valuable collection numerous papers with notations by Boettger. He made careful notes of each formula and the temperatures and duration of every firing. Under the date of January 15, 1708, he noted seven mixtures fired under high temperatures. On one paper (see inset) we read these mysterious words: ". . . has probas eodem die hora 12 impossuimus ignisque

Fig. 6. Vase of Boettger stoneware with black glaze and painted around 1715

datas, quo continuato usque ad horam 5 am vespertinum tunc crucibati extracti et patellulae inventae uti superiores ad signatum Numerum notatum envenies." These were the notations on firings of varying duration for one day, and he states that he was pleased with the success achieved with a few small bowls. The same paper also makes note that these bowls were white and transparent. We may consider this date, January 15, 1708, as the birth date of European porcelain, and this is why I dwelt extensively on Boettger's experiments.

This first porcelain, fired at 1,500 degrees, consisted of clay from Colditz and kaolin from Aue and was discovered in Dresden. Later, the flux was changed frequently, but the kaolin from Schneeberg in Aue remained constant.

On March 28, 1709, Boettger submitted a report to the King stating that he had discovered how to make white porcelain together with the finest of glazes and decoration that went with it, "which should at least be equal to the East Indian one." It took two more years before Boettger could put his invention to practical use (Tschirnhaus died on October 11, 1708). August the Strong founded the first European porcelain factory in the Albrechtsburg in Meissen in 1710, and it is in operation there to this day.

Some Technical Details

Porcelain is composed of the two basic ingredients —kaolin and quartz. Kaolin is a fatty clay, a decomposed product of feldspar or feldspar containing rock, equal to granite and porphyry. It is highly plastic and fireproof, which means that it does not melt at high temperatures, not even at 1,500 degrees. Feldspar and quartz are added for the purpose of counteracting too much "fattiness." The feldspar melts during the firing process and penetrates the pores of the clay. Feldspar and quartz have to be finely ground, and the kaolin is washed in water. Then follows the process of mixing the paste in distinct proportions, for which large vats are used. Finally, all water is extracted through the filter-press, and the product, the "cake," is left lying for a certain period of time.

The "cakes" are eventually put through a kneading machine to extract all remaining air. At this point the "cakes" are ready to use. The ware is thrown or turned on the potter's wheel, air dried, and fired first at 700 to 800 degrees. So-called saggers (clay capsules) are used for the firing, and they protect the porcelain ware from being soiled by fire and ashes. After the first firing the ware is slightly fragile and brittle and is now dipped into a glaze bath or sprinkled with glaze. The glaze is of the same composition as the porcelain "body," but it contains more feldspar, plaster, and alabaster, which are slightly liquid. The firing is done initially at 900 degrees and then follows the "sharp" firing at high temperatures of 1,500 degrees. The objects shrink in size by one third during the firing process. The porcelain is now pure white and translucent if it is not too thick.

Porcelain figures are treated in the same manner. The figure, which is modeled for the factory by either an independent artist or the modeler of the factory, is cast in plaster. Each limb, head, hat, body, etc. has to be cast separately. To make this possible, the model has to be cut into several pieces. Some porcelain groups consist of more than 200 separate pieces. When all parts have been formed and dried, the *Bossierer* (repairer) painstakingly joins them together with a liquid porcelain paste and creates the finished artistic figure, which is then fired as described above.

When the figures are painted they go through an additional process. There are two kinds of colors, the "muffle" colors (on the glaze) and the underglaze colors (mostly blue). In the "muffle oven" the colors fuse completely with the glaze.

THE GERMAN and AUSTRIAN FACTORIES

Meissen

Every monarch of the eighteenth century who was conscious of his responsibility to display the good taste befitting his high rank felt that it was his duty to own a porcelain cabinet. August bought the so-called Japanese Palace in Dresden-Neustadt and transformed it into his Porcelain Palace. Everything had to be made of porcelain—the tiles on the roof, the throne, the outer walls, the garden ornaments, the pulpit, the altar, the organ pipes. Each room had to be decorated in a special shade of porcelain. These fantastic plans, which were only partly realized, were to be fulfilled by Meissen, the mother of all European porcelain factories.

During the eighteenth century, unpainted porcelain was considered unfinished. Boettger had invented a few not very beautiful colors: a dull green, a lusterless yellow, brown, purple, gold, and a very beautiful luminous copper. It was Johann Gregor Hoeroldt from Jena who presented Meissen with its first lovely scale of colors. Samuel Stoelzel, the arcanist who had escaped from the Vienna porcelain factory, returned to Meissen with the young painter Hoeroldt. The punishment that threatened a traitor like Stoelzel was waived because Hoeroldt had brought some painted samples from Vienna which pleased the King greatly. Hoeroldt was hired in Meissen on May 22, 1720.

Little is known about his training. Accounts from Jena inform us that he had been in Strassburg in 1718, and that he was a painter of wallpapers in Vienna in 1719. He was married twice and was the father of twenty-one children. Hoeroldt was born in Jena on August 6, 1696 and died in Meissen on January 26, 1775. In Meissen he began to work with a vengeance. We know that Boettger already knew at that time how to produce a few colors, but they had no luster and were dull. The painters Richter and Mehlhorn worked on an underglaze blue, which later was to play an important role in Meissen (onion pattern). Hoeroldt's first color was iron-red. On December 13, 1721, it was noted already that the technique of painting had been improved to such a degree that "red and blue painted wares can be sent to Leipzig now." (The Easter and St. Martin's Fairs were being held in Leipzig.)

Hoeroldt himself gives the best description of the difficulties encountered in the production of his colors. The heading in his arcanum book reads: "True and Correct Description of the Enamels and Smelting Colors That I Have Found With God's Help and

That Are Being Used in This Royal Porcelain Factory. Also the Way Gold and Silver Should Be Handled. Recorded by Johann Gregorius Hoeroldt on December 24, 1731."

For curiosity's sake I shall quote here from Hoeroldt's arcanum book, where he gives his recipe for his blue-green color:

> How to make blue, so it will turn green. Take one part tartar and 1½ parts silica, crush fine. Mix these two materials and put in a smelting pot. Set it in a kiln and a fine white glaze will develop. Crush this fine and keep for later use. Take cobalt —three or four pieces—fire in hot kiln. Mix with flux and the cobalt will separate from the slag. Crush fine. Take one part of this, add five parts of flux of Menninge and two parts tartar glaze, mix well together and melt again. Take out of the smelting pot and crush fine. Take one part of this blue and mix it with two parts green. Rub it together and it will become a pleasing blue-green or steel green.

It is hard to imagine the enormous amount of work and knowledge that went into the manufacture of colors.

The income from the factory amounted, even in 1721, to 11,368 thalers, and the inventory had a value of 10,000 thalers. Hoeroldt began to instruct the painters and apprentices under him. Engravings and models to be copied were bought outside the factory. Even in 1723, newspapers warned of imitations of Meissen porcelain.

By 1725 Hoeroldt had succeeded in producing porcelain colors of great luminosity. They are exquisitely shiny and brilliant. According to August's demands, much was painted in the "Indian manner." Hoeroldt had painted wallpapers in Vienna, and he knew his chinoiserie. These pieces belong to the loveliest examples coming from Meissen. The paintings were inspired by accounts of voyages and by the illustrated reports from Jesuit missionaries in China. But there also was the Chinese and Japanese porcelain that had been imported on the ships of the seventeenth-century trading companies. There were fantastic birds fighting with each other and figures in bizarre garments wandering gracefully through Chinese pavilions decorated with tiny bells. Europeans of the eighteenth century were delighted with "Indian pavilions." Everything coming from the Far East was regarded as a charming curiosity.

A very good example of Hoeroldt's own chinoiserie on porcelain is a tea pot (Fig. 7) made from the porcelain of Boettger's time. It shows an unreal world inspired by a free-ranging and joyful imagination.

A marvelous tall vase (Fig. 8) with raspberry background, Indian flowers, and Chinese figures is also the creation of our artist from Meissen, Hoeroldt. A party of Chinese figures is seated around a table listening to guitar music. Meissen promoted this Chinese fashion until 1735–1740, when it was replaced by contemporary images.

As early as 1725, Hoeroldt had—aside from his chinoiserie—copied the scenes of his environment. He decorated a tankard with colorful princely "divertissements," as the eighteenth century called them (Fig. 9). Ladies in deep decolletage are seated at the game table—a scene well familiar to the artist —and playing whist. One couple, in majestic posture, is strolling toward the background. It was believed that August II could be recognized in the figure of the gentleman embracing one of the many maids of honor.

Hoeroldt's first colors are quite typical: deep brown, light green, blue, purple, and a deep iron-red. Yellow is missing. There are also towering steel-blue clouds. The painting, an excellent example of Hoeroldt's art, is framed with an underglaze blue line and a gold border. The intricate red and gold scroll frame points to the period between 1724 and 1725.

Around 1730 August ordered a second table service decorated with the Saxon and Polish coats of arms (Fig. 10). The Polish-Lithuanian coat of arms is painted in two iron-red fields, and under the purple and ermine electoral crown, in the center field, appears the coat of arms of Saxony. (In 1725 the crossed swords in the crown were selected for the mark of Meissen porcelain.) On the plate is a design of "Indian" flowers and rice reeds. This service has frequently been called the Coronation Service, as it was thought to have been ordered for the coronation of August III. However, this information is not based on fact.

Hoeroldt chose a thirteen-year-old boy as his first

Fig. 7. Tea pot. Boettger porcelain. Painted by Johann Gregor Hoeroldt with chinoiseries. Meissen, 1724

apprentice. He was the son of the shop assistant in the Dresden porcelain warehouse belonging to the *Hoffaktor* (Court Agent) Chladni. After he had observed the boy for five months, Hoeroldt and the boy's father agreed that Johann Georg Heintze was to stay in Meissen as a painter's apprentice for five years. Father Heintze had to furnish the bed linen and clothing. Hoeroldt gave him his promise that the boy would receive a thorough training in the art of painting with porcelain colors. Thus Heintze became the first, and as Hoeroldt said later, the best painter in the factory. In the roster of workmen of 1731 Heintze is listed as "painter of fine figures and landscapes, earning the high salary of thirteen thalers a month."

The story of his life can be told in a few words, as

Fig. 9. Tankard. Painted genre scene by Johann Gregor Hoeroldt. Meissen, 1725

it was typical of so many porcelain workers. In 1730 Heintze and three others were under suspicion of having painted porcelain at home without permission. Investigations revealed that he had received the green color from Master Stoelzel; he made the purple color on his own. The "muffle" colors he bought outside the factory from the potter Pfenning. Since he was a good painter he escaped punishment. But he was taken to the notorious and dreaded fortress Koenigstein in 1748 without being informed of the charges against him. He was ill for a long time with a "chest ailment." On April 23, 1749, together with other imprisoned Meissen painters, he escaped from Koenigstein and fled to Prague and later to the

Fig. 8. Large vase with raspberry colored background. Painted chinoiseries medallions. Meissen between 1725 and 1730

Fig. 10. Plate with the Royal Coat of Arms of Saxony-Poland. Meissen around 1730

Holitsch faience factory. From there he traveled to Breslau and further to Berlin, where we lose trace of him.

Thus, Heintze shared the fate of many arcanists and porcelain workers who ran away because of unbearable working conditions and low pay. We shall see later that these deserters played an important part in the founding of other porcelain factories. The best known among them was Joseph Jakob Ringler from Vienna, who had a hand in the establishment of nearly all the German porcelain factories: Kuenersburg, Strassburg, Hoechst, Nymphenburg, Schrezheim, Ellwangen, Ludwigsburg, Fuerstenberg, and Berlin. His disciples, Niklaus Paul

Fig. 11. Coffee pot. Painted harbor scene with merchant vessel. Around 1730. Mark: Swords and golden number *39*

and C. D. Busch, played a role in the founding of the factories in Weesp, Closter-Veilsdorf, Kelsterbach, and Frankenthal.

The list of names of the Meissen painters of 1731 is long, and only a few exceptionally able artists can be discussed. We have already made the acquaintance of Heintze. Christian Friedrich Herold—no relative of Johann Gregor—signed a snuff box which he had painted at home. It is painted in the identical manner as the tall coffee pot (Fig. 11) with the harbor scene shown here. A merchant in a purple coat is engaged in negotiations with a "supercargo" (captain of a merchant vessel), who points to the sailing ships lying in harbor. In the distance are small houses and large boulders. The *Boettger Luester* (gold scroll frame) was used generously.

As an illustration of the working conditions, let us consider Johann Ehrenfried Stadler. He was paid poorly but was permitted to paint in the evening after work, and could therefore at times earn as much as twelve thalers a month. Social laws regulating working hours then were unknown in Saxony. It is easy to recognize Stadler's work. He framed his figures with iron-red borders and favored dark purple contrasted by iron-red. He painted in the *Inselstil* (island style), meaning that he placed his figures on an island. They usually carry parasols and fans. The lantern depicted here (Fig. 12) is an excellent example of his particular style, and his signature, JES, can be seen on a paper held by the small Chinese figure. Frau Menzhausen, curator of the Dresden porcelain collection, states that this lantern is mentioned in the inventory of 1721 as being an authentic copy of a Chinese lantern.

The most contested painter at Meissen, and probably one of the most important, was Adam Friedrich von Loewenfinck. In 1731, at the age of only seventeen and still an apprentice—although in his fourth year of apprenticeship—he painted multicolored flowers. He was permitted, as were a few other apprentices, to paint after working hours. There is an extensive body of literature on Loewenfinck, and researchers and experts are at odds over his reputation. One can distinguish his paintings without difficulty, as he had a distinct style of his own. Some porcelains and faiences are signed "AFL" and "FcL," and they resemble drawings found in the Meissen archives (Fig. 13). These drawings were undoubtedly done by Loewenfinck, and the upper left drawing appears again on one of his plates. Here we see for the first time the so-called "Fabeltiere" (fable animals), fabulous, unreal creatures adorned with fantastic tails and antlers. They are painted in rich colors, in striking contrast to the white porcelain.

On October 3, 1736, Loewenfinck fled Meissen on a stolen horse belonging to the baker Starke. When he reached the faience factory in Bayreuth, he explained the reasons for his flight in a long letter: he had been treated harshly by Hoeroldt, and the distribution of work had not been fair. Escape from Meissen was considered equal to the desertion of a soldier and subject to severe punishment. Since Loewenfinck was only too well aware of this, he changed his place of employment again and again. From Bayreuth he went to Ansbach, then to Fulda, and later to Hoechst, where the porcelain factory of the same name was founded by him in 1745. Hoechst had only produced faiences up to that point. After an argument with his patron there, he moved on to Strassburg-Hagenau, where he died in 1745 as the director of that city's faience factory. This was typical of the roving life of a very accomplished artist who, as has to be pointed out, did not know the secret formula for the production of porcelain.

Both brothers of Adam Friedrich von Loewenfinck, Carl Heinrich and Christian Wilhelm, were also taught to paint in Meissen. After 1733 the overall direction of the factory came under Count Heinrich Bruehl, and Count Sulkowski supervised the work on the Japanese Palace. Both Bruehl and Sulkowski ordered large services for themselves.

The most important one of these was the "Swan Service" for Bruehl. It had 2,200 individual pieces and was decorated with the coat of arms of Bruehl and Kolowrat-Krakowski (Fig. 14). "In splendor and merry-making Count Bruehl was equal to the King, and his fascinating and entertaining conversation made him indispensable" (Dr. Rueckert). This service illustrated elements of marine life, symbolized by swans and herons among reeds, and dolphins, mermaids, crabs, snails, seashells, and the sea god Neptune with his trident. The designs for this service were made by Meissen's master modeler, Johann Joachim Kaendler. This gigantic order kept all the factory's modelers occupied.

A later biographer of Bruehl, Aladar von Boroviczeny, wrote about the Swan Service: "More often than once did the Meissen porcelain Swan Service exert a subtle influence on the foreign dignitary's mood, when he had to be wooed at the dinner table. Bruehl's hospitable and splendid residence echoed the outdoor festivities by torchlight, the playing fountains and the overwhelming spectacle of fireworks which had been arranged by August the Strong on the banks of the Elbe in Zeithain."

Many others aside from the King ordered their services in Meissen. The ones for which correct dates are available are: Althann-Daun (1731); Berntorff

Fig. 12. Lantern. Painted by Johann Ehrenfried Stadler after a Chinese model. Meissen around 1725

Fig. 13. Designs by the Meissen painter Adam Friedrich von Loewenfinck. Archives of the Meissen factory, around 1735

(1735); Clemens August, Prince Bishop of Cologne (1735); Contarini (1735); Falletti (1740); Ferrero (1740); Frederick the Great (1761); the King of France (1745); Moellendorf (1761); Hennicke (1735); Hoyn-Werthern (around 1735); Muenchhausen (1740); Pisano-Cornaro (1740); the Russian Empress (1755); Seydewitz (1732); and Hoepfner (around 1735). The last service on this list is the only one which, according to the coat of arms, was not dedicated to a noble family.

Besides these armorial services, Meissen delivered innumerable other services throughout the eighteenth century. As a rule, they consisted of one hundred to two hundred pieces, but tea sets for one or

Fig. 14. Tureen belonging to the "Swan Service" made for Heinrich Count Bruehl with coats of arms of Bruehl and Kolowrat-Krakowski

Fig. 15. Platter. Painted with a scene after Watteau. Meissen, around 1745

two persons and even individual pieces were much in demand. Around 1740 the "Indian" decor and chinoiserie were replaced by scenes taken from Watteau, Lancret, and the French engravers of the eighteenth century (Fig. 15). Simultaneously there was a change in the flower design. The first *Deutsche Blumen* (German flowers) appeared after 1740. They were copied from woodcuts, with and without shadows such as those in the Dutch paintings of the seventeenth century. After 1750 there was a preference for the common flowers of field and garden. The shapes of the ware as well, which during the rococo period tended to be exaggerated, sometimes almost bizarre, became more subdued and rational.

So far I have spoken exclusively about the production of services. However, they were not solely responsible for Meissen's fame. Figures and groups of figures of great beauty were shaped by skilled modelers. Until Boettger resurrected it, no specifically ceramic sculpture had been in existence since the sculpture of antiquity. The first Meissen figures in stoneware and porcelain were imitations of Chinese and contemporary objets d'art. There was also the work of unknown but quite accomplished artists: a large crucifix, figures of the Italian *Commedia dell'Arte,* a small statue of the King, and some works

Fig. 16. Tureen. Model by Kaendler, 1738. Originally designed for the Queen

in relief. It is possible that a few artists from Dresden of the circle around Permoser supplied some models. A few small figures were modeled by Georg Fritsche and Johann Christof von Lueck.

The first significant modeler was Johann Gottlieb Kirchner, twenty-one years old. He was hired at a salary of 220 thalers on April 29, 1727 but was dismissed again one year later. We know a few clock mountings by him, painted with chinoiserie by Hoeroldt, and there are also some chandeliers, washbasins, boxes, and "other models of pleasing invention," as they are called in the archives. In 1730 he was rehired, this time at a salary of 300 thalers. It had not been possible to find a better master modeler. The large animals are from this period, and they represented a noteworthy technical achievement. We have only to consider what it meant to fire these porcelains in a kiln. One tiger, which Kirchner worked on for three months, was 2½ ft. (75 cm) tall (Fig. 17).

Kirchner encountered a formidable artistic rival in Johann Joachim Kaendler. They did not get along. Since Kaendler had shown excellent proof of his skill, Kirchner was dismissed in February 1733. Kaendler continued to work in the factory from 1731 up to his death in 1755. The Kaendlers came from

Fig. 17. Tiger. Model by Johann Gottlieb Kirchner, 1733. Height 2 ft. 6 in. (75 cm)

Planitz, near Zwickau. Father Kaendler was a clergyman in Fischbach, where Johann Joachim was born on June 15, 1706. Here he grew up with twelve brothers and sisters. The boy was given a humanist education, as was customary for the son of a Lutheran clergyman. Kaendler's grandfather and great-grandfather had been stone cutters. This proved decisive for the future profession of Meissen's master modeler. In 1723 he became a pupil of Benjamin Thomae, who together with Permoser worked on the ornamental sculptures of the Dresden Zwinger. August II watched the young sculptor at work and found him able enough to entrust him with the responsibility for the artistic direction of the new factory,

Fig. 18. August the Strong, King of Poland and Elector of Saxony. Model by Kaendler, around 1732

even though Kaendler was not at all familiar with the problems of porcelain. Nevertheless, he started to work at the Meissen factory on June 22, 1731.

The monthly report for June on the "modeler Kaendler," sent to Dresden by the porcelain factory's director, announced "three different models. In particular, one large eagle and further pieces being completed in clay, to be cast in plaster and finished in porcelain." Kaendler himself describes this first creation with the following words: "A large eagle which together with the pedestal and outspread wings measures two yards less five inches in height."

In the months to follow he modeled a heron that was 2½ ft. (75 cm) in height, a Boy with Goat, a Vulture with Dead Parrot, and a life-size peacock, 118 cm in height. These were Kaendler's very first models. He had proved his artistic competence.

It was only natural that he should model a statue of August the Strong (Fig. 18). This figure was completed in 1732. The strong colors and the special way in which the palm design on the purple garment has been traced with the tip of his brush handle point to his early period.

To illustrate the immensity of his creative urge, I shall enumerate the models he executed in one year, 1733: Indian Lion; Oriole; Woodpecker; Falcon with Lark; Peacock on a Tree Trunk; nine different bulldogs; Indian Bird; King of the Vultures, life-size; Vulture with Dead Parrot; Arara Leaning Against Tree; Indian Sheep; African Ducks; Parrot; Small Lynx; Small Goat. All animals were life-size. This was only one year's work for Kaendler, truly an impressive accomplishment. Much of it has been preserved for us and the factory in Meissen still has his plaster molds.

A standing candelabra supported by three elephant heads (Fig. 19) is a typical example of the baroque period, when everything exotic and outlandish was treasured. Kaendler's own description of this candelabra, which is dated June 1735, reads: "One Table Candelabra in Indian Manner, one and one half levels, which is rich in ornamentation, the pedestal consisting of three elephants heads, their trunks resting on foliage and scrolls. On this pedestal there are three pagodas, each one holding two graceful candle holders. Under these pagodas three Indian Birds are resting on a canopy, their necks bent backward, each of them holding a candle holder for illumination. The candelabra can easily accommodate ten lights. The candle holders held by the pagodas may be exchanged according to one's desires, since there are two of them. One has the shape of a graceful branch overgrown with leaves and flowers. On it sits a young dragon, holding the candle holder on his head." The brass mounting was added in Dresden in 1737.

One of Kaendler's famous figures portrays the last court jester of Saxony, Josef Froehlich. Since the Renaissance it had been customary for princes to keep jesters at their courts. August II employed two, the *Hoftaschenspieler* (Court Magician) Froehlich and the *Kammerkurier* (Courier Chamberlain) Schmiedel. The King had supplied Froehlich with as many as ninety-nine jester's costumes. Froehlich was intelligent, well liked at the court of Saxony, and held in high esteem by the King. Froehlich, a wealthy peasant who had come to Dresden via the court at Bayreuth, owned his own residence in Dresden and had a carriage and a servant. His constant adversary was Baron Schmiedel, who was inclined to be of a melancholy disposition. Froehlich, on the other hand, was said to have died one day in Warsaw of laughing too much. The King ordered several porcelain portraits of Froehlich, and Kaendler made the first model in September 1736 (Fig. 20): "One Josef figure in clay, altered and improved, so it can be cast anew."

The actors of the *Commedia dell'Arte,* whom we know as Harlequin, Columbine, Pantalone, Dottore, and Scaramouche, were also immortalized in Kaendler's figures. His colleagues, too, worked on a collection of comedians. Kaendler must have been well acquainted with these improvising artists of the stage, and they inspired his imagination. The Indiscreet Harlequin (Fig. 21) may have been done around 1740. This group is a typical document of its time. One only needs to observe the movements and expressions of the various figures. Kaendler's crinoline groups have become world famous, and the Lady with Cavalier (Fig. 22) is one of the best.

Kaendler completed around 900 masterpieces. An equestrian monument of August III, larger than life, on which he worked for many years, was never completed, although 800 details were finished. The Seven

Fig. 19. Candelabra with three elephant heads. Model by Kaendler, June 1735. Mounted in brass around 1737. Height 1 ft. 8 in. (55 cm)

Years' War and lack of funds prevented its final completion.

The large sculptures for the Japanese Palace were too much to be mastered by Kaendler alone. On April 18, 1735, the forty-year-old sculptor Johann Friedrich Eberlein was engaged as Kaendler's *Adjuvante* (assistant). Little is known of his previous history except that he made good models. By May he had produced two swans and one Owl with Chamois Goat for the Japanese Palace; these were followed in June and July by a lamb, a stork, a turkey, and two sparrows, all life-size. But Eberlein also worked on porcelain merchandise, on tableware and figures. The pair of dancing peasants (Fig. 23), done in 1737, and a pair of Dutch figures, also dancing, are among the best of Eberlein's models. His work resembles Kaendler's but can be distinguished by the slanted eyes of his figures, which lend them an Oriental expression.

Three further colleagues of the great master modeler were Johann Gottlieb Ehder, Peter Reinicke, and Elias Meyer. Ehder seldom worked independently; he had less talent than the other two. Unlike Ehder, Reinicke demonstrated diligence and skill and was therefore entrusted with important work, such as the 16 in. (42 cm) high portrait busts of popes, ordered by Cardinal Albani, and a series of portraits of the Hapsburg emperors, dedicated to the Empress Amalia. The extensive collection of Paris street criers was done jointly by Kaendler and Reinicke. The drawings for these had been sent from Paris by Huet. Reinicke's most important work is a collection of fifteen Italian comedians, done after engravings by Louis Riccoboni in Paris for the *Histoire du Théâtre italien*. It had been ordered by the Duke of Weissenfels. And last but not least was a charming series of four Chinese groups designed by Reinicke, who died in 1768.

The factory employed another young sculptor, Elias Meyer. Born in 1724, Meyer came from Erfurt and took the place of Eberlein, who had died after a long illness in 1749. Meyer, who worked quite independently, was a master of mythology and allegory. He gave his figures strangely elongated bodies and small heads, but he had the reputation of a skilled artist. Frederick the Great persuaded him to come to Berlin in 1761. In his place the factory hired Carl Christof Punkt, who, however, died in 1765.

All these artists contributed to make Meissen famous all over the world, and their masterpieces are worth their weight in gold today. The great period of Meissen's porcelain sculpture came to an end with Meyer's departure. Although Kaendler was still working, a new era was approaching, and porcelain sculpture was not valued any more as it had been before.

After the Second Silesian War, political conditions in Saxony became more settled, but the Seven Years' War (1756–1763) dealt the factory some heavy blows and threatened its existence altogether. The unexpected invasion of Saxony by Frederick the Great—August III and his ministers had fled to Poland—brought the work of the porcelain factory to a standstill. The Prussian King gave orders to have the workers and clay transported to Berlin. As a precaution, the kilns in the Albrechtsburg were destroyed and the kaolin was spirited away. The Berlin porcelain manufacturer Wilhelm Kaspar Wegeli appeared in Meissen. Under the protection of the King of Prussia, he had managed his factory for four years, but rather unsuccessfully. Frederick ordered thirty cases of porcelain to be dispatched to Berlin. The factory's premises in the Albrechtsburg were sealed, the stock of merchandise offered for sale.

Three men who remained behind saved the Meissen factory under the direction of the Queen. They paid the Prussians 190,000 thalers, although this meant a heavy financial sacrifice. They were *Kommerzienrat* (Councilor of Commerce) Helbig, owner of the Dresden branch, Carl Heinrich Schimmelmann, and *Armeelieferent* (Purveyor for the Army) Count of Bolza.

Under the pretense that they had to replace some parts for certain dinner services, the factory started to work again with a few men. The orders from the King of Prussia became more and more exorbitant. He expected all deliveries within the shortest period of time—breakfast sets, snuff boxes, the Festoon Service, large groups representing continents and the creative arts, theatrical figures, etc. At his orders, the kilns were rebuilt, and the responsibility rested on Kaendler alone, since Hoeroldt had fled to Frankfurt. Frederick tried to persuade Kaendler to come to Berlin, but he remained loyal to Meissen. Two talented landscape painters, Borrmann and Boehme,

Fig. 20. Court Jester Froehlich. Model by Kaendler. 1733. Cast in 1740

Fig. 21. The Indiscreet Harlequin. Model by Kaendler, 1740

and the mosaic painter Klipfel left for Berlin—a heavy loss for Meissen. At least the factory, the pride of Saxony, had been saved from complete destruction, but the European market was almost non-existent by now.

Then the sculptor Victor Acier, born at Versailles in 1736, was called to Meissen. He was at once offered a salary of 400 thalers a year with a pension of 400 thalers after fifteen years. He worked quite independently of Kaendler, but Kaendler still enjoyed the highest respect and even in old age continued to be a most creative and productive artist. Acier worked together with the former repairer Johann Karl Schoenheit, who later became a very capable

Fig. 22. Lady and Cavalier Kissing Her Hand. Model by Kaendler, 1737

modeler. Acier created a new style, the so-called Louis XVI. He was well suited for this, since he had come from Paris. His models are not among the best that Meissen had to offer. Instead of the crinoline ladies and comedians, upright citizens made their appearance, and the former shepherds and shepherdesses were replaced by sentimental lovers. The vigorous creations of Kaendler were swept away, and although some figures still stood on adaptations of the rococo pedestals, these were soon to be dispensed with, too.

The services were now given the Louis XVI decor with scenes from Angelica Kauffmann and from Goethe's *Werther,* and they were painted in sepia,

Fig. 23. Pair of Dancing Peasants. Model by Johann Friedrich Eberlein, around 1735

in monochrome only. Acier retired in 1781 and was succeeded by Christof Gottfried Juechtzer, who led the factory through the transition into the nineteenth century. Kaendler and Hoeroldt both died in 1775, and with them died the glorious period of Meissen porcelain. Its fame has survived to this day.

Production continued throughout the nineteenth century, and since 1945 Meissen has been in operation as a nationalized enterprise.

Because of its significance as the cradle of European porcelain, I have discussed Meissen and its talented artists, sculptors, and painters at great length. The beauty of its earliest masterpieces well deserves this.

Vienna

DU PAQUIER

The victorious wars against the Turks and the consequent dismantling of the Vienna city fortifications ushered in a period of splendor for the old imperial city. The architects Johann Bernhard Fischer von Erlach and Johann Lukas Hildebrand created a city panorama that still fascinates visitors. Artists from every part of Europe made pilgrimages to Vienna and offered their best talents to the city. Emperor Charles VI issued a proclamation on June 2, 1717, which assured support and protection to all those who would bring benefit and success to Austria through the establishment of factories. The imperial *Hofkriegsagent* (Army Contractor at the Court) Claudius Innozens du Paquier from Trier, originally a Dutchman, tried to heed the wishes of the Emperor, and he was convinced that a porcelain factory was indispensable to the "splendor and dignity" of an imperial court.

It was no secret that true white porcelain was being manufactured in Meissen. Du Paquier had entered into Austria's service in 1708 and since 1717 he had labored unsuccessfully on the invention of porcelain. On May 17, 1718, the Emperor granted him the "privilege" for the exclusive manufacture and sale of porcelain in all the provinces of the imperial domain. This document also mentioned the army contractor Zerder and the merchant Martin Becker, who no doubt were the patrons.

Du Paquier could hope to be successful only if he succeeded in recruiting workmen from Meissen. The Austrian ambassador at the court of August the Strong, Count Virmont, came to his aid. He engaged the wandering arcanist Christof Hunger, who was a friend of Boettger. Du Paquier called for him in person in October 1717. Hunger was anything but an expert in the production of hard porcelain. Since his own relations with the King were at times rather tenuous, Boettger sent his half brother Tiemann to Vienna with the kiln designs. Du Paquier detected a ray of hope. In spite of Christof Hunger they failed.

Only after the arrival in Vienna of the Meissen paste mixer and kiln master Samuel Stoelzel, who had been wooed by the musician La France, did the experiment succeed. Stoelzel had been promised 1,000 thalers a year, free lodgings, and a carriage with coachman. It was he who fired the first true porcelain in Vienna, in 1719. He ordered kaolin from Aue, the same deposit from which Meissen received its clay. Clays from Debrecen and Passau had been used previously, and neither yielded fine samples; the porcelain had been of a greenish or yellowish color. The first pieces which were fired without mishap were two cups. They are today in the Museum for Arts and Crafts in Hamburg and are dated 1719. The etched dedication reads: *"Gott Allein die Ehr und Keinem mehr"* (Honor to God Alone and to No Other).

The factory was in the quarter of Rossau, in the Schmiedgasse, now called Liechtensteingasse. When in April 1720 his payment was not forthcoming, a repentant Stoelzel fled back to Meissen, taking with him the eminent painter Johann Gregor Hoeroldt. Before they left they smashed everything and ruined the paste. Hunger mentions this sad incident in a letter: "These godforsaken and dishonorable men stole the colors because up to now they did not know in Meissen which colors would appear blue, green, red, or yellow on porcelain." That he was not so wrong is apparent from Meissen's rapid progress after Hoeroldt's arrival.

The factory recovered despite the enormous loss of 15,000 thalers. There were now twenty people employed in the new building in the Porzellangasse. Lack of funds still remained the main problem. A certain Christof von Gudenus lent the factory 12,000 florins, and the Emperor demanded that the city of Vienna take shares in the porcelain factory. This brought in another 18,000 florins but tied to the money was the obligation to divulge the arcanum to the Emperor and to submit accounts to a regular examination. Funds were to be raised by lotteries as well.

In 1729 du Paquier organized a *Glueckshafen* (Harbor of Good Luck), as lotteries then were called. The drawing plan of the *kaiserlich priviligierten Porcelain-Fabric* listed 2,000 prizes. At another lottery in 1735, each lottery ticket cost one ducat. We do not know the results. The principal buyer of the merchandise was the Emperor, who presented his protégés with porcelain and gave it to foreign dignitaries. At times the pieces were mounted in gold.

Du Paquier specialized in hunting scenes. These services were decorated in Schwarzlot and gold. Some services were made for the Emperor, for Liechtenstein (Fig. 24), and for Trivulzio. The hunt was regarded as one of the most magnificent *divertissements* at the Viennese court. At dawn soldiers marched through the city with bullhorns inviting the population for these occasions. The public and the nobility assembled in the *Hetzamphitheater* near the Kaerntnerthor. The nobility were seated on a raised tribune, while below wild animals roared behind iron bars. They were chased through the arena by dogs, and "His Most Christian Majesty" shot them down. This entertainment may have inspired du Paquier to embellish his tableware with game and wild animals. There was a large service with hunting scenes among the prizes of the *Kraenzelschiessens* (another lottery). The painters mainly worked from models supplied by Elias Ridinger of Augsburg, the famous engraver of animal scenes. The Austrian Museum for Applied Art still has several volumes of these engravings, which had belonged to the porcelain factory.

Fig. 24. Platter from the Liechtenstein service, painted in black and gold with game animals. Vienna, du Paquier, 1735–1740. 13 in. (34 cm) in diameter

Besides Indian flowers and hunting scenes, the factory imitated Chinese and Japanese porcelain from Imari and Hizen. According to the accounts of travelers to China (Neuhof in 1666, Kirchner in 1667, and Montanus in 1697), scenes painted in black existed there even in the seventeenth century. For the most part, however, the early Viennese porcelain, just as the Meissen porcelain, is decorated with landscapes and stylized flowers, at times with shadows, as can be seen in the woodcuts of the seventeenth century.

What could one buy at du Paquier's establishment? Everything that belonged in an eighteenth-century household. Washbasins with ewers, breakfast sets for one or two persons, called solitaire or tête à tête, coffee pots and tea pots, tureens with two handles shaped like tigers, bottles for smelling salts for the young ladies who were inclined to faint whenever the occasion demanded it, flower vases, butter dishes, tea containers, hot water containers, and hundreds of everyday objects, executed artistically. For twenty-five years the forms hardly changed. The following figures were offered as well: butter dishes in the shape of turtles at sixteen florins a piece; Indians at eighteen florins; a crucifix with three figures at 300 florins; a cane handle for one florin; two tea cups at 1 florin 30 xr (Kreuzer) to 2 florins 30 xr; two *Commedia dell'Arte* figures; a Lady with Moor, after the Meissen model of 1735. I believe that the pair of lovers shown here (Fig. 25), to this day of unknown origin, actually are a du Paquier model of the period between 1735 and 1740. The best preserved example of early Viennese work is the Dubsky room, formerly in the castle of Count Dubsky in Bruenn but today in the Austrian Museum in Vienna (Fig. 26). Everything was made of porcelain: candelabras, vases, and the plates that were set into the walls.

To conclude this chapter on the first period of Viennese porcelain, I would like to acquaint the reader with some of the artists and painters of the factory. We already know Hunger, who prepared the paste. His place of birth was Weissenau in Thuringia, and he came to Meissen via Frankfurt in 1717 but traveled on to Vienna the same year. He is de-

Fig. 25. Pair of Lovers. Vienna, du Paquier, around 1735–1744

scribed as a somewhat dubious character. Soon after Stoelzel's escape, Hunger left Vienna too and went to work for the brothers Vezzi, who had opened a porcelain factory in Venice. Later his name appears again in Sweden, Copenhagen, Berlin, and St. Petersburg.

The painter Karl Wendelin Anreiter of Zirnfeld in Hungary was of far greater importance than Hunger. He had moved to Vienna after his marriage in 1724. He was one of the foremost painters in the factory, and at times he signed his work with his full name. In 1737 he went to Doccia near Florence to work at the newly established factory of the Marchese Ginori. Ten years later we find him in

Nymphenburg. His son, Anton, was superintendent of the painting department in the Viennese porcelain factory from 1754 to 1801. The Vienna marriage register lists one Anton Schultz in 1726, and he appears there as "painter of the porcelain factory." He was still painting in Vienna in 1743, but then changed over to the Prince Bishop's faience factory in Fulda.

In all probability, Josef Philipp Dannhoefer also learned to paint in Vienna. Much has been written about this eighteenth-century painter. He had a skilled hand and changed his place of employment frequently. I would like to mention these places briefly to illustrate the roving existence of a man who was attracted by promises from one place to another, but who continued to move on because of the precarious situation most factories found themselves in. The factories where Dannhoefer worked as a painter were: Bayreuth (1737–1744), Abtsbessingen (1744–1747), Hoechst (1747–1751), Fulda (1751–1752), Hanau (1753–1757), again Fulda (1757–1758), Schoenbornslust (1758), again Hoechst (1759–1760), Ludwigsburg (1762–1790, the year of his death). Dannhoefer knew how to paint faiences as well as porcelain.

Also deserving mention is Jakob Helchis, whose stay in Vienna cannot be easily defined. However, it is assumed that he painted there as early as 1730, perhaps not as an official factory painter but as a so-called *Hausmaler* who secretly painted porcelain at home.

The following names of painters were found in church registers: Boehme, Klinger, Lacher, Lemercier, and Mayer. No records of their individual activity can be found, however. Du Paquier managed his establishment with these artists until 1744, when the factory was bought for the crown by the Empress Maria Theresa for the sum of 55,000 florins. With this sale the first period of the Vienna porcelain factory came to an end. Du Paquier stayed on as director for a short time. He died on December 27, 1751.

THE IMPERIAL FACTORY

Maria Theresa entrusted the overall direction of the factory to the *Blancodeputierten* (Deputy with Unlimited Powers) Franz Xavier Mayerhofer. The twenty craftsmen who remained modeled and painted as they had done before, with the one exception that every piece now had to be marked with the Austrian coat of arms. The old porcelain from du Paquier's time was auctioned off. This "inconvenient ware" was now disposed of by the sale of 6,000 lottery tickets.

The factory came to new life when three new painters—Busch, Klinger, and Hitzig—arrived from Meissen. Since Saxony found itself in the throes of the Second Silesian War, they preferred escape to arrest. Busch was the son of the Meissen *Porzelain-offizier* and was trained as a painter. But after barely three years he ran away from Vienna to Nymphenburg, and from there again to Bayreuth, Paris, and Kelsterbach. It is obvious that he was not merely a painter, but had knowledge of the arcanum; that is, he knew how to produce porcelain. Wherever he went, the firing of true porcelain suddenly became feasible. Johann Gottfried Klinger was more stable. Before he died in Vienna in 1781, he had already won the reputation of a skilled flower painter in Meissen. Ferdinand Teuscher's specialty was Dutch landscapes. Samuel Hitzig left again in 1750, although he had been selected for the position of teacher of the young apprentices. His departure was a painful loss for the factory, but he was soon replaced by an equally skilled painter, Johann Sigmund Fischer.

The register lists 250 painters and gilders who worked in the factory until it closed in the nineteenth century. Some stayed for a few months only, others for decades. The polychrome painter Josef Drexler worked there from 1746 to 1804, and the excellent painter of fruit and flowers, Franz Sennes, started at the age of seventeen in 1747 and died as *Schreiber* (calligrapher) in 1804. To expand production, a second kiln hall was built for 4,000 florins, accommodating two new kilns and several workrooms. Anton Anreiter von Zirnfeld was chief painter and later kiln master. He was assigned to determine the wages for each painter and to distribute the work. By 1750 the staff had grown to fifty, and by 1761 to as many as 140 men. The yearly income in 1767 was between 120,000 and 170,000 florins.

One man who may have worked as an apprentice

Fig. 26. A view of the Dubsky cabinet. Du Paquier, around 1730

during du Paquier's time was Joseph Ringler, born at St. Stephan on July 12, 1730, the son of the school's headmaster. "Because of his close friendship with the director's daughter," according to an account dated 1750, "the twenty-year-old Ringler came into the possession of the secret of how to make true porcelain and what clays were being used." Who was the daughter who stole this secret from her father's desk? In 1750, according to his own account, Ch. Ludwig von Lueck was *Oberdirector* of the entire factory. Since Lueck was born in 1710, his daughter, like Ringler, may have been twenty years old.

As the bearer of the secret, Ringler was now assured a hearty welcome at all princely courts. From

Vienna, Ringler went to Hoechst. In 1752 he was in Strassburg, where he instructed Paul Hannong in the firing of porcelain. One year later he appeared like a savior in Neudeck-Nymphenburg, where, after many previous failures, porcelain began to be manufactured from then on. Ringler also stayed for a short while at Memmingen, Schrezheim, and Ellwangen, until he found a permanent position as director in Ludwigsburg on February 16, 1759. He died there in 1804. The arcanum books which he left shall be discussed further in the chapter on Ludwigsburg.

Vienna modeled more than tableware. After the middle of the eighteenth century, figures and groups were in great demand. Johann Jakob Niedermayer became master modeler in 1747 and was responsible for the entire artistic production. He had formerly worked at the art academy as a drawing teacher. The majority of figures of the rococo period from 1747 to 1781 were done by him, until he was replaced by Anton Grassi. His first task was to copy as many Meissen groups as he possibly could. This is why there are so many typical Meissen models by Kaendler bearing the Vienna mark! Another modeler who had been in Meissen previously was the already mentioned Johann Christof von Lueck. He created the new rococo style that followed the baroque. He did not stay for long, and we know that in 1751 he applied unsuccessfully from Hamburg for a position at Fuerstenberg. Josef Dangel, Josef Gwander, and Leopold Dannhauser should be mentioned as repairers who remained loyal to the factory for fifty years.

Fig. 27. Pianist, Vienna around 1770, and Singer, Vienna around 1750. Model by Niedermayer

What was the work of a repairer in a porcelain factory? Repairers had to be skilled craftsmen with a great deal of artistic knowledge. As has been explained before, it is not feasible to cast a complete figure in one piece. The repairer must assemble the figure from the many individually-cast parts. For control purposes each piece is impressed with its own mark, but this process differs from factory to factory.

The inventory listed hundreds of individual figures and groups for sale, and the selection of the Vienna factory was vast: soldiers, *Cris de Vienne* (colorful characters who called out their wares in the streets of Vienna), artisans, graceful figures of crinolined ladies, a singer holding notes and baton accompanied by a piano player (Fig. 27). The singer was probably done by Niedermayer around 1750, while her accompanist must have been modeled ten years later. The piano player was "repaired" by Josef Dangel, the singer by Anton Payer. Everything and everybody who formed a part of the city panorama was being reproduced in porcelain.

Anton Grassi was the master modeler after 1778. The Family in Spanish Costume (Fig. 28) falls into this late period. Grassi's later models approached the neo-classical style, which was not well suited to the old porcelain. There were attempts to cash in on the vogue for imitations of Greek and Roman sculpture. In 1767 Johann Winkelmann wrote in *Remarks Concerning the History of Antiquity* that those porcelain figures modeled after the classical statues "contributed to a significant degree in elevating a sense of beauty and the level of taste." The eighteenth century was coming to an end and with it the era of splendor for European porcelain.

Fig. 28. Family in Spanish Costume. Vienna around 1780. Model by Anton Grassi

Thanks to Konrad Sorgenthal, who was the factory's director from 1785 to 1805, an important new period began for the manufacture of tableware. He sold off the enormous stock which had become unfashionable and which nobody wanted to buy any longer. It became a luxury to retain the ninety-seven polychrome painters and fifteen blue painters with their combined salaries of 20,000 florins, and all but fifty were dismissed. However, the best painters were kept. Plans were made for the modernization of the factory, but Emperor Josef gave orders to either sell or lease it. As a first step, all the porcelain was auctioned off, and on July 20, 1784, the factory itself came under the auctioneer's hammer, although the Emperor's advisers had counseled him to save it for the city of Vienna. The total assets of the factory, including its stock and all the buildings, came to 300,000 guilders. It was offered at auction for 45,000 florins, but no buyer came forth. Thereafter the factory remained the property of the empire, but it was necessary to take the most incisive measures of reform. It was Sorgenthal who was responsible for their execution. By 1791 the number of painters, previously reduced to fifty, was increased to 196. Sorgenthal died on October 17, 1805, after forty-seven years of loyal service. He died a disillusioned and disappointed man, as his Emperor had never shown him the recognition he deserved. With Sorgenthal the eighteenth century, the century of porcelain, came to an end.

Hoechst

THE FAIENCE FACTORY

Adam Friedrich von Loewenfinck of Fulda arrived in Mainz early in 1745 with the plan of convincing his Holy Highness, Elector Johann Friedrich Karl von Ostein, to build a porcelain factory. To win his Highness's favors, he had sent him a set of beautifully decorated vases from Fulda before his arrival in Mainz. Loewenfinck knew very well that only the establishment of industries could mitigate the ravages of the Thirty Years' War, and the provinces under the rule of the church were no exception. We have already met Adam Friedrich von Loewenfinck, who in 1736 fled from Meissen to Bayreuth on a stolen horse. From Bayreuth he paid his debt of fifty florins and even paid for the horse, but in spite of that he was not forgiven by Meissen and escaped arrest only by moving on to Frankfurt.

In 1741 we encounter him again in Fulda, where Prince Bishop Amandus von Buseck confers the title of Court Enameller on him in recognition of his artistic achievements. It was in Fulda that he produced his "faience porcelain" for the first time. It was made from particularly fine clay with a tin glaze.

Loewenfinck found the suitable clay for his faience production in Weissenau near Mainz. He built his kilns in a long-abandoned brewery with the assistance of the kiln master Heinrich Eberhard of Fulda. He had to pay 140 florins rent a year. However, not more than six months later, Loewenfinck broke his contract and left Weissenau, because two merchants from Frankfurt advised him to move his factory to Hoechst. They promised to give him all their assistance in that city.

These patrons were Johann Christof Goeltz, citizen and merchant of Frankfurt, and his son-in-law, Johann Felizius Clarus. They were the owners of an enterprise which supplied the raw materials to various glassworks. In addition, Goeltz was manager of the mirror factory at Lohr am Main. Both were going to take equal shares in the new porcelain factory.

One needed permission from the Elector to open a porcelain factory. On February 8, 1746, Goeltz and Loewenfinck submitted a plan stating that Hoechst was most suitable because it contained a large residence standing half empty with a storage yard that would serve the factory well. They stipulated that there should be no second porcelain factory in the country, and that the factory workers should be granted their personal freedom. The wheel on the princely coat of arms was suggested as a mark. Eight days later, the church authorities agreed but added that "there was to be consideration of religion."

Goeltz and Clarus confirmed their agreement by a contract two weeks later, and everything was ready. The first firing, on December 7, 1746, yielded no satisfactory results. The glaze was quite useless. Two weeks later Loewenfinck was satisfied with the second firing, but the painting had to be improved. His

Fig. 29. Wall candelabra, in faience. Hoechst around 1746–1747. Period of Adam Friedrich von Loewenfinck

assistants were: Johann Heinrich Eberhard of Fulda, kiln master; Johann Gottlieb Becker of Meissen, modeler and repairer; Philipp Magnus Bechel of Fulda, painter; Johann Heinrich Heller of Fulda, former and day laborer; Georg Friedrich Hess of Fulda, polychrome painter and repairer; and Johann Lorenz Hess, painter from Fulda. With these six craftsmen Loewenfinck started his faience plant, which he boastfully called a porcelain factory.

Two years later he increased his staff by ten more men, including his brother Christian Wilhelm and Dannhoefer from Vienna. By the end of 1748 he worked with thirty-five men. Together they manufactured faience tableware. The wall candelabra

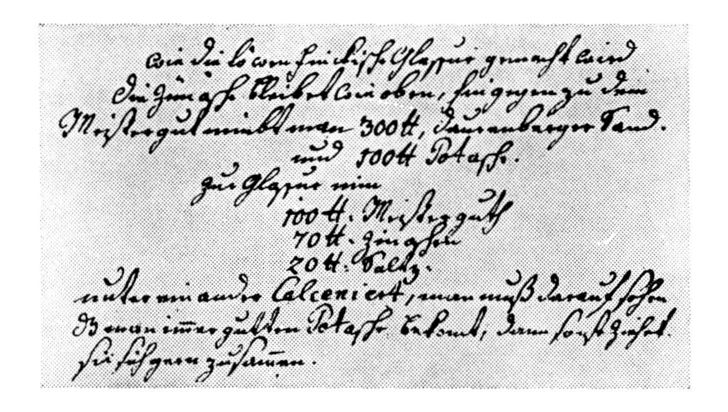

(Fig. 29) is one of Loewenfinck's first examples from the period between 1746 and 1747.

Reproduced above is a page from Ringler's arcanum book describing the composition of Loewenfinck's faience porcelain.

Dissatisfaction among the workers and disagreements between them and the director troubled the happy relationship between Loewenfinck and Goeltz to an unbearable degree. The hatred resulted in a duel between Dannhoefer and the floral painter Rothe, and the Viennese was seriously injured. After a lengthy trial Rothe was sentenced to leave the country immediately, and Dannhoefer, too, was sent away. Since Loewenfinck and Goeltz were unable to come to an agreement, the Elector, on February 13, 1749, gave orders for Loewenfinck to leave the factory within twenty-four hours.

It should be added that Loewenfinck's art and craftsmanship were above slander. It was only natural for him to defend himself as best he could against unjust—or just—accusations. This is where he failed and the reason why he was dismissed by the Elector. However, as was proven by subsequent developments, the Elector was ill advised. After Loewenfinck's departure, and despite a loyalty declaration signed by all workmen promising to serve Goeltz "loyally and diligently," the faience factory's fate was sealed. Twenty-eight men had signed the oath, but within one year ten had departed. To forestall complete collapse, Goeltz sent for a man from Vienna who knew how to manufacture hard porcelain: Johann Kilian Benckgraff.

THE PORCELAIN FACTORY

On June 7, 1750, Goeltz informed the Elector that he had engaged a "man of years" from Vienna, one who was "quiet and virtuous" and who had no intentions to travel further. He would "with the help of God bring order to the factory." Forty-two years old, Benckgraff was "a man of years" in the eighteenth century. However, he was not able to produce true porcelain on his own and he sent for the kiln master Joseph Jakob Ringler from Vienna. With Ringler's help they established the third true porcelain factory, after Meissen and Vienna.

The first kiln was ready by November 1750 and Hoechst fired its first porcelain the same month. Ringler's reputation in Hoechst appears to have been very high. On the occasion of the baptism of little Johannes Dantz, Ringler's godchild, the priest made the following entry in the baptismal records: *"Dominus Josephus Rinckler de Vienna hujatis fabricae porcellaneae inserveniens."* The word *Dominus* was reserved exclusively for the city's dignitaries. Ringler left Hoechst and moved on to Strassburg either at the end of 1751 or in the beginning of 1752.

The first porcelain workers under the direction of Benckgraff in 1750 included eleven painters, two repairers, five modelers, one turner, one *Ofenmacher* (builder of kilns), and one kiln master. To them we owe Hoechst's first tableware and figures. To this period belongs an exquisitely-painted basin and ewer (Fig. 30) executed by a floral painter, most likely Johannes Zeschinger. The clay merchants Philipp Stallmeier in Hafnerzell and Franz Orthner in Griesbach supplied Hoechst with kaolin. Benckgraff made notations of the arcanum which are preserved in the archives of the Fuerstenberg factory.

Benckgraff shared the same fate that befell Loewenfinck and Ringler. Goeltz now felt capable of manufacturing hard porcelain without the help of Benckgraff's arcanum, and he thought that he could dispense with this costly director. He found all sorts of transparent excuses to make life unbearable for Benckgraff. Goeltz's son withheld the keys and barred his entry to the factory. This was not the end of the affair, and court proceedings were started which filled 150 pages. The charges were that Benck-

Fig. 30. Ewer and basin, probably painted by Johann Zeschinger. Hoechst around 1750–1755

graff had sent a small barrel of porcelain to Berlin, and had thereby given away the arcanum, that he had made copies of the kiln construction, and that he had not recorded the arcanum. After long and superfluous negotiations—all charges were lies—Benckgraff was dismissed. He departed for Fuerstenberg together with his son-in-law, Zeschinger, and the painter and repairer Feilner.

Affairs in Hoechst now went from bad to worse until Goeltz went bankrupt in 1756. He addressed a memorandum to Chancellor Bentzel asking for assistance. The management of the factory had depleted his resources, but he still felt that its continued operation offered advantages to the archdiocese. The value of the finished merchandise was higher by 50 per cent than the expenses, he said, and the standstill of production would inflict hardship on the citizens, since artisans and innkeepers were dependent on it. Also, he stated that the factory provided a place of employment for the children of Hoechst's citizens. The Elector had no intention of closing the factory. He asked Goeltz to come to Mainz to discuss the matter, but Goeltz declined, saying that he suffered from gout and swollen legs. He hoped that the Elector would take over the factory. There was enough porcelain paste to last for another thirty years. These lies were most transparent, and an inventory of the factory proved that there was clay to last for four years and that the workmen had not seen any pay for an entire year. To alleviate the most pressing needs, the Elector sent 700 florins. Three hundred florins were needed to pay one week's wages; the supply of fuel was dwindling; and the three factory horses were starving and there was no more hay. There was no shortage of orders, however, and Monsieur Bassin sent models and sketches from Paris.

On May 15, 1756, the customs clerk Scheppler received a secret order to retain the porcelain factory for the Elector. Work was to be resumed at once. From the city of Frankfurt, the Elector demanded that Goeltz be put under lock and key and

Fig. 31. Group representing Spring. Hoechst, April–June 1758. Model by Johann Friedrich Lueck

that his remaining property be confiscated: "It becomes more obvious from day to day how shameless and wicked is the behavior of this Goeltz. Instead of thinking of how to indemnify us for what is our due, he underhandedly collects the active debts which rightfully belong to the state." Goeltz had embezzled 74,000 florins belonging to the Elector and had stolen 34,000 florins from the communal coffers. On August 15, 1757, Goeltz's residence, including all the porcelain found in it, was auctioned off. Shunned as an impostor, Goeltz died the same year. He had paid for his crimes against Loewenfinck, Ringler, and Benckgraff.

An applicant to manage the factory was sought

through an announcement in the *Frankfurter Ober Post Amtszeitung* of September 28, 1756. Nobody applied. Therefore the factory came under the management of the *Pfandamtsdeputierten* (bailiffs) Johann Heinrich Maas and Vogt. Johann Adam Bergdoll kept the accounts. He tried to manage the factory with fourteen men at a cost of 1,812 florins a year, and faience production was discontinued altogether. In spite of everybody's efforts the factory was closed in December 1756 and most of its craftsmen left Hoechst. In 1757 work came to a complete standstill. There was some stock left, consisting mainly of faience ware, valued at about 18,000 thalers.

The Hoechst porcelain factory was reopened in April 1758. It is surprising that most of the workers and artists returned. From April 5 to June 4, the two famous Meissen modelers, Johann Friedrich Lueck and his brother Karl Gottlieb, also worked in Hoechst. For a number of years they had been working in Meissen under Kaendler as formers, and they felt capable of doing independent work. The group shown in Figure 31 proves that they were right. This allegory of spring demonstrates Johann Friedrich Lueck's skill. With its lively rocaille pedestal, the group is typical of the rococo period.

A list of the inventory gives us a good idea of the factory's production. The merchandise included flower pots, mustard pots, warming plates, cups, bowls, plates with molded decorations, chocolate cups, night lamps, porcelain baskets, thimbles, soup tureens, vegetable platters, sugar bowls, bases for knitting bags, parrots, canaries, etc. We can deduce that production was brisk and that it was possible to buy everything a substantial household was supposed to own.

THE FACTORY OF JOHANN HEINRICH MAAS

After March 6, 1759, Maas was the only entrepreneur of the porcelain factory. He was particularly privileged, since the Elector had presented him with the entire factory. Everything necessary for production—kilns, grinding mill, tools, molds, paste, and colors—was put at his disposal free of charge. He had to pay neither rent nor duty. The privilege granted him by the Elector was drawn up in the same manner as the previous privilege granted to Goeltz. The list of workers shows the following names:

Aest, repairer
Russinger, modeler
Ruppel, former
Schneider, former
Lambrecht, turner
Heckel, Niklaus, glaze grinder
Dantz, kiln master
Bart, turner of saggers
Winterstein, painter
Heckel, Jakob, painter
Heckel, Jr., apprentice painter
Magnus, apprentice painter
Strentz, former
Ostern, day laborer

In the faience department there were:

Stattmayer, arcanist
Caspar Huber, turner
Abraham Ripp, turner
Franz Birkensee
Georg Kraemer
Josef Attiné
Michael Schukart
Johann Ruppel
J. Ph. Dannhoefer

The nine faience workers were dismissed in the middle of August, since Maas no longer manufactured faiences.

Elector Friedrich Karl von Ostein died on April 4, 1763. He had contributed significantly to the upkeep of the factory. His successor was Emmerich Joseph, Baron of Breidbach-Buerresheim.

As early as 1764, Maas had informed the Elector that it was impossible for him to keep the factory without risking the loss of all he owned. Since the new Elector wanted to keep the factory in operation, the Mainz commission of commerce met in 1765. Newspapers carried reports on "The Progress of the Hoechst Porcelain Factory of Mainz." Plans were drawn up for a company of shareholders buying twenty shares at 800 florins each. The shares could be inherited and divided. The Elector promised to support the factory with special favors. We are not informed whether anybody answered this announcement, but a share belonging to Count Eltz, dated July 16, is still in existence.

Herr and Frau Maas agreed to manage the factory a few months longer. After an interruption of five months the factory resumed production. The participants—i.e., the workmen—had to sign an oath promising that they would stay at least one year. The nineteen workmen who signed this loyalty oath included Laurentius Russinger, a modeler, and Johannes Angele and Johannes Zissler, painters, to mention the best of them. The Elector advanced the factory 2,000 florins. The young Webel, nephew of *Kommerzienrat* (Councilor of Commerce) Webel in Frankfurt, was appointed director. The factory operated exceptionally well under Herr and Frau Maas's management. The following figures and groups were offered for sale:

Genre scenes	Boat with Boatman
Large pastoral group	Italian Musicians
Hunting group	French Comedians
Turkish emperor	Group of cobblers
Garden scene	Skaters
Apollo group	Woodsman
Fountain of Love	Scissors grinder
Ox hunt	The seasons
Savoyard	Pilgrims

The factory became the property of the joint stockholder company on August 20, 1766. On this day Herr and Frau Maas resigned. Among the stockholders were many eminent persons of the region. Twenty shares had been distributed altogether, but some had been given as payment for debts incurred by the factory. For instance, Webel in Frankfurt, who had delivered raw materials to the factory, was owed so much money that his shares brought in merely 8,100 florins instead of 16,800.

Director Webel drew up an inventory listing thirty-eight different kinds of decorated figures and groups and thirty-six unpainted pieces. Each piece was priced according to the decoration.

	unpainted	*painted*
Large Hunting Scene	15 florins	45 florins
Fountain of Love	25 florins	55 florins
Large Pastoral Group	20 florins	36 florins
Scissors grinder	15 florins	20 florins
Ox hunt	16 florins	30 florins
Wigmaker	4 florins	87 florins

The most expensive were:

Diana with Stag	85 florins
The Dog Wedding	86 florins
Chinese Emperor	80 florins
Lion Hunt	65 florins
Globe with Children	55 florins

Compared to the wages the workmen received these prices were very high. The average income was between ten and twenty florins a month.

Webel was director for a short time only. The reason for his dismissal was characteristic of the period: He had a love affair with the sister of the painter Oettner, "whom the director wishes to marry under false pretenses declaring his intention to convert to the Catholic faith." Uncle Webel in Frankfurt was beside himself. He hoped "that this disgraceful creature would choke to death during childbirth and that God would inflict his just punishment on this whoring and shameful behavior." Webel's place was taken by the old Hornung, who was no great genius. The possessions of former director Webel were auctioned off in the factory.

The hiring of Johann Peter Melchior as master modeler was the most significant event of the year 1767. Russinger went to Guttenbrunn. The bookkeeper Johann Kauschinger was promoted to director in 1768 with instructions to "devote himself to a pious, modest and elevating Christian life." He was urged to see to it that his workers without exception executed their duties diligently and efficiently. He was informed of his duties toward the factory in twelve written paragraphs, one of which stated that clients had to be kept informed of the durability and beauty of Hoechst porcelain. Similar instructions were drawn up for the inspector. Merchandise which did not sell promptly was auctioned off.

Melchior was Hoechst's most famous artist and assured its fame for posterity. Melchior was born in 1747. The biographer Michel Oppenheim writes that even in early youth he decorated benches and floors with figures of men and animals. Having lost both parents in childhood, he kept body and soul together working as a shepherd. Soon he was dismissed because he did not watch the cattle but spent his time drawing and modeling instead. Through the kind intervention of a cousin he was apprenticed to a sculptor. Melchior studied with several artists, some of them quite famous. He became so well known that sculptors competed for his services when he arrived in Cologne. The Elector of Mainz appointed him master modeler of his porcelain factory when he was only twenty years old, and on February 1, 1770 he was made court sculptor.

Fig. 32. Group of children: the Shepherd Crowned with Flower Wreath. Hoechst before 1770. Model by Johann Peter Melchior

Melchior created 300 different models in Hoechst. A few he signed with his full name. The charming little Shepherd with Floral Wreath (Fig. 32) is his, as is the large and exceptionally well executed representation of Amyntas and Sylvia, characters taken from a novel by Torquato Tasso and a painting by Boucher (Fig. 33). The Amyntas and Sylvia cost 30 florins in 1771 and was the second most expensive piece sold in Hoechst. Melchior left Hoechst in 1779, went to Frankenthal, and then moved to Nymphenburg in 1793. He died there in 1822. Not only was he an outstanding modeler of porcelain, but he was equally famous for his sculptures in stone and even for his political writing.

A new stockholders' meeting was convened on April 22, 1771, and the outlook was not encouraging. The workmen were owed 4,000 florins. They had not been paid for a long time. The factory had not profited much from the sale of lottery tickets, and the stockholders were urged to buy fifty lottery tickets each for resale. There was a total deficit of 39,165 florins.

The meeting passed varying resolutions for reorganization which, if realized, would have amounted to no more than a drop in the bucket. Another proposal was to open new branches in Hamburg, in Aachen, at the Schwalbach and Schlangenbad spas, and perhaps also in Wetzlar, the residence of many foreign dignitaries.

The Dutchman Brauwer in Rotterdam was a good client of the factory. He initiated a new lottery sending a down payment of 6,000 florins on a large shipment of porcelain. Orders for porcelain amounting to 30,000 florins arrived from England, Holland, St. Petersburg, Hamburg, Aachen, Cologne, and Koblenz. To fill these it became essential to engage more repairers, but the request was refused from above. Permission was granted to hire only two new repairers and a former, Kilber. Between September 1, 1772 and May 31, 1773, the factory produced porcelain at a cost of 13,000 florins but sold only 3,500 florins worth. There was still a small credit balance. A new inventory for the year 1773 lists hundreds of figures and, for the first time, also biscuits (work without glaze).

The factory operated with sixty-four workers. They were not paid badly, but quite frequently they received only a fraction of their salary. For instance, Melchior was promised forty-five florins but only received 28 florins 30 xr. Others fared worse: Distel, painter, promised 32 florins 45 xr, received 11 florins 20 xr; Sommerlad, painter, promised thirty-three florins, received 2 florins 12 xr; Spengler, apprentice painter, promised twenty-nine florins, received nine florins; Heckelmann, repairer, promised 18 florins 20 xr, received 1 florin 20 xr. It remains a mystery how anyone could have lived on two florins a month at a time when a small pig cost 2 florins 30 xr, and it is not surprising that all porcelain workers were heavily in debt. They usually ran away under cover of darkness and looked for work elsewhere when the debts grew to be over their heads.

One of the best painters around 1775 was Johann Melchior Schoellhammer, whose name is not mentioned in the Hoechst archives but who, according to a report by his contemporary Alexander von

Fig. 33. Amynthas and Silvia. Hoechst before 1770. Model by Melchior after a painting by Boucher

Humboldt, painted in Hoechst and Frankenthal. He also painted in Ansbach between 1758 and 1807. The signature "Schell" is on several large vases, a breakfast set for two, and a chocolate pot. He must have been extremely capable because, compared to the usual work done at the factory, these paintings clearly stand out by their exceptionally fine and colorful treatment.

Victor Louis Gerverot is another roving artist and arcanist who seems to have worked twice in Hoechst. Between these two periods he worked at Sèvres, Niderviller, Ludwigsburg, Ansbach, Fuerstenberg, Frankenthal, Weesp, Schrezheim, Oude, Loosdrecht, Lane End, Cologne, Brussels, Muenster, again in Fuerstenberg, and Hildesheim—a true vagabond. In Hoechst, a service with genre scenes in the most exquisite colors was painted by him.

The plan to raise 4,000 florins, as resolved at the stockholders' meeting in 1773, could not be realized. Obviously, citizens and patrons would not invest too much confidence in the fragile enterprise. Conditions in the factory were precarious. The Elector appointed an investigating commission to examine the state of affairs. When the Elector died in 1774, the company was in debt for 17,330 florins. The new Elector, Friedrich Karl Josef, Baron von Erthal, stated that the stockholders should either liquidate the factory or raise the funds for its maintenance. Franz Josef Weber was appointed to prepare an estimate of its financial solvency. The results of his investigation were so discouraging that the Elector dissolved the joint stock company on December 30, 1778 and Rief, a member of the commission, was appointed administrator of the Electoral Factory.

There was no shortage of proposals on how to improve the operation, but Rief was a disloyal civil servant and only damaged the factory even more by his fraudulent schemes. The ensuing trial lasted from 1780 to 1783. Rief had embezzled 1,347 florins which he had to pay back. In addition he nad to return 156 florins to the exchequer and he was stripped of his title of *Hofkammerrat* (Councilor of the Exchequer).

After his dismissal work was resumed until 1793, when after a new estimate suggestions were made again to close the factory. This was actually done in 1796. The debts had now mounted to 85,000 florins. War precipitated the complete breakdown. In 1792 Frankenthal had been occupied by the Hessians and Prussians. General Custine retreated to Hoechst but spared the factory. The buildings were still intact at the end of the nineteenth century.

In 1796 the factory was advertised in the newspapers. Its value was estimated at 900 florins, the mill at 150 florins, and the surrounding land at 350 florins. Since no agreement on the purchase price could be reached among the interested parties, every deal fell through. When the *Oberamtschreiber* (Chief Recorder) Heim came forward with his offer, the entire factory including buildings, land, and stock were sold to him for 6,700 florins. He had permission to sell the stock "and dispose of it freely at his pleasure."

Thus ended the fluctuating history of Hoechst's porcelain factory. It was founded at a time when porcelain represented the splendor of princely courts and it came to an end when the ravages of war ruthlessly swept away the ancien régime.

Fuerstenberg

The history of Fuerstenberg's porcelain factory is interesting because the state archives in Wolfenbuettel have preserved 14,700 pages of its records for the years 1753 to 1800. With the exception of Meissen, Fuerstenberg is the best documented of all the eighteenth-century porcelain factories. The reader cannot expect equally magnificent masterpieces in the styles of Kaendler, Melchior, or Bustelli, but the tableware was painted exceptionally well, and the plastic art gives evidence of some very skillful modelers.

Adam Friedrich von Loewenfinck had promised Hoechst's Elector that he would manufacture true porcelain. However, only Benckgraff and Ringler succeeded. The same drama was repeated in Fuerstenberg, when Johann Christof Glaser, an artful swindler, assured Duke Carl von Braunschweig that he knew how to produce hard porcelain. The Duke gave him his Castle Fuerstenberg in 1744, and the *Hofjaegermeister* (Court Master of the Hunt) von Langen took over the direction. It took eight years for von Langen to realize that the Duke and he had been duped.

Funds for the new factory came in slowly. The Duke sent von Langen 210 florins, and thirty of these were used by Glaser to pay off some old debts. The arcanist needed workers to prepare his porcelain paste. In 1751 we find the names of Johann Michael Heyne from Kassel as turner, Johann Georg Paland, repairer, and formers Johann Christof Pfeffel and Ferdinand Junge. After the first firing the Duke found that the paste was not pure, the glaze unsatisfactory, and the colors were quite impossible. In 1753 von Langen gave the following verdict: "Glaser is a miserable painter; everything else he has produced is useless, and whatever he still plans to do is a lie. We are as far removed from true porcelain as brass is from gold."

It became feasible to manufacture true porcelain only after Fuerstenberg succeeded in recruiting the well-known director of the Hoechst porcelain factory, Benckgraff. It was the traveling clay merchant Buerger of Montabaur who was successful in this. And it took him longer than one year. On February

3, Benckgraff finally agreed. He could not leave Hoechst right away but gave instructions on the construction of the kiln and where to order suitable clay. On May 6 he arrived in Fuerstenberg in the company of his daughter, his son-in-law, Zeschinger, Simon Feilner, and the floral painters Geisler and Zissler. Benckgraff died four weeks later. As a wedding present he had passed on the arcanum to Zeschinger, and the production of porcelain did not have to be interrupted.

The first firing took place in October 1753, and the Duke found the results excellent. To make quite certain that Zeschinger and his family would remain in Fuerstenberg after Benckgraff's death, they had to swear "by God and the most holy, pure and blessed Mother of God, and all Saints." There was great rejoicing at court over the successful results of the experiment. The Duchess sent her servant to the factory carrying a box with broken porcelain, asking to have it melted down and to have new porcelain made from it.

The first assistants in 1753 were three workmen at the kilns, the master modeler Feilner, three formers, the repairer Franz Joachim Hess, five painters, and two men who washed the clay and prepared the paste. Among the best were the floral painter Kind, arcanist and painter Metsch, and landscape painter Ostertag. Jeremias Pitsch made the molds and Johannes Zeschinger was the finisher.

During the Seven Years' War the factory, now in full swing, went through trying times. In July 1757 the French invaded Fuerstenberg, and while they spared the factory, they looted and set fire to the homes of citizens, including the factory workers. Business suffered considerably during this unsettled period. Thirty craftsmen were sent away to the faience factory in Braunschweig and to the academy of art. At the end of the war in 1763, conditions gradually became normal again. The Duke had paid his workers reduced wages all through these hard times: Eisentrager six florins; the other painters—fourteen of them—between six and four florins a month; Guenther, the former, six florins, and the other formers five florins a month; Paland and Schnede each seven florins; the other turners only four to five florins; both Brenner and Boehme, as well as Erbrecht, had to be satisfied with six florins.

The modeler Feilner had created the first Fuerstenberg figures and for this he received a yearly salary of 500 florins. The plate with eight engraved coats of arms shown here (Fig. 34) should be dated between 1755 and 1758 and is no doubt one of Feilner's models. The magnificent decoration was probably painted by Nerge or Oest after an engraving by Amiconi, *Astronomy*. The signature "j" tells us that the cast was made by Ferdinand Juergens.

When Zeschinger escaped from Fuerstenberg on July 7, 1756, it almost led to an official rift between Duke Carl von Braunschweig and the Elector of Cologne, Clemens August. Johannes Quitter from Westphalia and a dismissed officer, Pierson, had talked Zeschinger into moving to Bonn to build a porcelain factory there for the merchant Kaysin. Zeschinger had consented. During the investigations that followed, he pleaded that he had left merely to get away from his mother-in-law, the widow Benckgraff. She had remarried and had passed on the arcanum to her new husband, and besides had converted to the Protestant faith. She had done him much harm. She was a wicked woman, and he had been degraded to the position of a lowly finishing painter. If a man like von Langen had gone back on his word, he, Zeschinger, was entitled as well to look for employment elsewhere. Zeschinger was apprehended in Paderborn and put under arrest. The ensuing legal deliberations delayed matters for weeks. Finally, on January 28, 1757, the Elector of Cologne decided to release Zeschinger and his family immediately. The next day they arrived in Fuerstenberg, but Zeschinger was sent to the workhouse. However, he was spared the mandatory punishment of twenty lashes.

A personnel roster of 1757 illustrates how the factory had progressed in spite of the war. There were now eighty-nine workers. After von Langen's departure for Copenhagen, *Berg-, Huetten- und Oberforstkommissaer* (First Commissioner of Mines and Forestry) Bernhard August Trabert became director. He was a man of intrigues, as became apparent later. Simon Feilner remained master modeler, Christian Gotthelf Beuchel chief painter, Johann Georg Paland master turner, Ferdinand Juergens foreman of the formers, and Johann Werner Hopstock kept the books. The factory operated success-

Fig. 34. Plate with eight engraved shields, painted by Nerge or Oest after an engraving by Jakob Amiconi: Astronomy. Fuerstenberg 1750–1755

fully with these men, and yet new difficulties arose again and again. There were at times no funds for the wages, or a drought immobilized the grinding mill. In spite of everything, Fuerstenberg manufactured magnificent porcelain. Feilner issued regular reports. The most important models were his figures of miners and of the *Commedia dell'Arte.* His designs were always submitted first to the Duke, who would give his approval. To his groups belong the Cavalier and Lady (Fig. 35), adapted into a candelabra and painted by either Hintze or Jungesblut.

A Johann Christof Rombrich of Blankenburg offered models of cane handles, clock mountings, and portraits. Since they were very successful in Fuerstenberg, he was hired as inspector and modeler, and Fuerstenberg never had a more prolific modeler. From 1758 onward, he modeled charming figures and groups. His most creative period falls between 1771 and 1780. One of Trabert's reports informs us that porcelain valued at 30,000 florins was produced in 1759. With the completion of six kilns it was planned to fire porcelain worth 57,600 florins.

Kaolin was brought from Passau, and after 1753 from Lenne. Between 1757 and 1777, Johann Friedrich Borchers, a pharmacist, manufactured the colors.

It is interesting to consider the training of the apprentices. A figure painter's apprenticeship lasted eight years, a landscape painter's seven, a flower painter's six, a repairer's eight, a molder's six, a turner's five. After the completion of the apprenticeship, the wages were rated according to its duration: Figure painter Nerge earned twenty-six florins per month; landscape painter Eisentraeger, fifteen florins; floral painter Zissler, twelve florins; repairer Leimberger, eighteen florins; former Keusch, ten florins; turner Schnoede, twelve florins; the wages, however, were never paid out in full. In most cases only half was paid and the balance carried forward as debit.

It may be interesting for the reader to get an idea of the workers' rights and duties. The Duke had drawn up the following rules:

> The worker must swear loyalty to the Duke and the factory.
> Respect and loyalty toward his superiors, as is deemed suitable of loyal subjects.
> No incitement against colleagues and superiors.
> The factory's secrets must not be given away.
> No worker can stay away overnight, nor travel without permission; if he does so nevertheless, he is to be punished.
> The worker is not permitted to get drunk as there is danger that "not being in possession of a rational mind" he might give away secrets.
> Whoever has debts must draw up a contract of settlement with his creditors; whoever gets deeper into debt and does not pay, must expect imprisonment with only water and bread.
> Working hours must be observed strictly. Work starts at six o'clock and lasts until eleven o'clock; in the afternoon, at one o'clock, ending at six o'clock. In summer work ends at four o'clock on Saturday afternoons. There is no work on Saturday afternoons during the winter months.
> Each one has to do the work that is assigned to him by the head painter and the master modeler.
> Smoking of tobacco is forbidden to the porcelain paste workers.
> The worker is permitted to send for a drink during working hours, but drinking parties are subject to punishment.
> When he is ill or disabled, the worker is cared for, and so are his wife and children; there are no deductions from his wages.

These were working conditions during the eighteenth century. A few are still valid today. Fuerstenberg is the only porcelain factory to pay sickness and disability benefits to its workers since its early days, without a charge.

What did Fuerstenberg produce around 1760? Everything for everyday use could be purchased from the factory: coffee and tea sets, chocolate pots, cups with ringed handles for shaky hands, so-called *trembleuses,* serving platters, plates with openwork borders, soup tureens, potpourri vases, *brûles-parfums* (incense burners) for sweet-smelling essences, fireplace ornaments, chamber pots for women and children, barber bowls.

In 1763 the Duke confirmed Trabert's promotion to the position of director with a salary of 400 florins a year. The yearly production came to almost 25,000 pieces of porcelain. Feilner invented a "baile" glaze (brown).

As in every other large factory, there was much coming and going in Fuerstenberg. The figure painter Andreas Philipp Oettner applied from Hoechst for a position and was engaged in 1766. He was a cultured man, a calligrapher of exquisite Latin letters. From Kassel came the turner Megis, while the turner Paland, who had been in Fuerstenberg since 1750, went to Kassel, where he was able to improve his position significantly as master turner. Repairer Kuenkler went to Berlin and from there to Thuringia. C. G. Albert, the best painter of birds, painted tableware at the academy in Braunschweig and according to Trabert was quite indis-

Fig. 35. Pair of Lovers. Modeled as candelabra. Fuerstenberg around 1760. Model by Simon Feilner

pensable. The painting on a tall vase with lid decorated with parrots and exotic birds (Fig. 36) was done by him. It is not a *brûle parfum,* as it lacks an openwork lid.

Meissen felt the competition from Hoechst, Vienna, and Fuerstenberg more and more keenly. It countered by cutting its prices. In the *Hanover Magazine* of 1770 there appeared an article on Fuerstenberg's porcelain factory, stating that "it appears that there are too many factories, since there are some in England, France and Italy, and others in Germany besides those in Berlin, Dresden and Fuerstenberg, as well as in Vienna. Moreover, within the last two or three years, one factory has been

Fig. 36. Vase with lid. Decoration with birds painted by C. G. Albert. Fuerstenberg around 1765. Height 15 in. (37.5 cm)

established in Switzerland at Zurich which produces exceptionally well-turned-out merchandise, decorated most tastefully." These laudatory remarks will be recalled in the chapter dealing with the Zurich factory.

Between July 1766 and May 1767, Fuerstenberg had expenses amounting to 18,700 florins, while income from the sale of porcelain reached the sum of 12,700 florins only. The Duke made up the deficit. In his opinion the factory's accounts could be balanced only by dismissing some workers. The first in line was Feilner, who was reproached for no longer following instructions and for being lazy (we know around one hundred models made by him!).

These unfounded accusations were invented only to save the 720 florins which he received yearly in addition to his rent-free lodgings and fuel. Trabert dismissed him at the end of December 1768. Feilner found employment two years later at the porcelain factory in Frankenthal where he made an important contribution and was awarded the title of *Hofkammerrat* (Councilor of the Exchequer). His models were held in high esteem. It was not feasible to dismiss additional workers immediately because there was no money to pay what was owed to them. At this point Director Trabert died and the Duke appointed *Bergrat* (Commissioner of Mines) Kaulitz in his place.

After Feilner's dismissal another modeler had to be found. Although Rombrich was still working, he could not cope with the work by himself. In 1769 an artist from Paris, Desoches, came forward. He had a certificate from the *Academie Royale de Sculpture,* confirming that he had worked for one year under Mignot. His samples pleased Kaulitz so much that he wrote to the Duke: "His work progresses speedily, and it is light and modern." Desoches was hired as repairer with a monthly salary of sixteen thalers. He left not more than five years later.

Anton Carl Luplau, son of the *Herrschaftlicher Fasanenmeister* (Master of the Pheasant Hunt) in Blankenburg, was a capable modeler, too. He came to the factory as an apprentice in 1759, finished his apprenticeship after eight years, and received a yearly salary of 120 thalers, exactly one third less than Desoches. Luplau went to Copenhagen in 1776. The quality of his work was equal to that of Feilner and Desoches.

One of Luplau's models—No. 223, "A Russian Canteen Proprietor"— is shown here (Fig. 37). As I mentioned before, the modelers and painters mainly worked from engravings, and this model is a good example of that process. Luplau's figure is done after an engraving by Le Prince, one of a series of Russian street vendors (see illustration p. 54). Luplau created a very faithful three-dimensional version of the picture. The finisher, too, did his best to portray the humble condition of his subject.

In 1770 the finances of the factory had not improved and expenses still exceeded income by far.

Fig. 37. A Russian Canteen Proprietor. Fuerstenberg, 1772, Model No. 223 by Anton Carl Luplau, after an engraving by Le Prince from the second series of Russian street vendors

To balance the two the Duke again gave orders to dismiss more men. This, however, was never done. The factory employed seventy-six craftsmen who received a total of 5,600 florins a year in salaries. Added to this were the expenses for clay and paint. The production of saggers alone cost 662 florins, the

operation of the kilns 832 florins, the polychrome painting 2,500 florins—a total expense of 12,917 florins. But the income from sales was only 8,000 florins. Four thousand florins had to be contributed by the Jews who, in return for obtaining a marriage license, had to buy porcelain. They were permitted to resell it. In 1770, 35,450 pieces of porcelain were manufactured. Prospects were poor, wrote technical manager Kohl, because Meissen, Ludwigsburg, and Frankenthal sold porcelain for 300,000 florins by lottery; these factories undercut Fuerstenberg's prices.

Kohl was a man with a tender heart. He regretted that "poor workers should be sent away in the midst of winter." The workers lived in deepest poverty. In their distress they dared send a letter to the Duke, which all of them signed. They asked to be paid up to date, as they had not been paid for the last five quarters, except for a small consolation sum in October which their creditors had snatched from them greedily. The missive, dated December 6, 1773, contains a moving message: "Our condition is growing more pitiful by the day; our misery and our need increases daily: we can hardly buy bread for our wives and children. We humbly implore Your Excellency to graciously and promptly heed our demands, including, however, the money owed us this Christmas quarter, since we no longer see a way out of our misery and poverty and will have to perish otherwise."

The molder of tableware, Johann Georg Pentzer, who had worked in the factory for seventeen years, asked the Duke to be permitted to continue to work, as his wife was pregnant again and he already had five children: "For this mercy, I myself and my wife and children will without fail send our prayers to heaven daily as long as we live."

I have included these original contemporary quotations because they are vivid documents of the eighteenth century. The Duke's answer was the dismissal of twenty workers. They received their wages up to Easter. Nothing was left for the others, since the court revenues had been scanty as well. Why was the factory kept in operation? Kohl offers some answers here, too: Some workers were in poor health or they had many children who would die of starvation. A porcelain factory was indispensable to a prince's glory. It had up to now given work and bread to the population. Other factories, too, had to contend with difficulties, and they continued nevertheless. In the end, Kohl would not dismiss anyone, with the exception of a few men who left on their own accord.

Some painters were sent to the academy in Braunschweig where they painted multicolored porcelain. The floral painters remained in Fuerstenberg.

In 1767 sales had gone back by 70 per cent. The porcelain's quality did not improve during the last quarter of the eighteenth century. Statistics recorded by the kiln master show a doubtful state of affairs. In 1775, 13,664 pieces of tableware were fired. Of these, 1,627 were perfect, 6,035 only average, 3,607 poor, and 2,395 were useless—*cassiert,* as the expression went. Of the 29,081 pieces of tableware painted in underglaze blue, 875 pieces were good, 14,502 average, 9,839 poor, and 3,846 useless. In spite of these unpleasant statistics the year 1775 was not too bad, and for the first time there was even some profit. Against expenses of 9,320 thalers, income from sales entered by cashier Reichart showed a sum of 10,650. The polychrome workshop in Braunschweig, too, had worked quite profitably.

According to the personnel roster of 1781, there were nine painters and two repairers working in Braunschweig; in Fuerstenberg there were five blue painters, ten molders, seven turners, four men preparing the paste, four men at the kilns, two turners of saggers, and seven unskilled laborers, a total of fifty workmen. The establishment had been greatly reduced. Desoches had left in 1774, Luplau was in Copenhagen, and only Rombrich remained. Carl Gottlieb Schubert was now modeler. It seems that he started to work in Fuerstenberg in 1778, but not much is known of his activity there.

On May 12, 1795, the much traveled painter, director, and founder of factories Victor Louis Gerverot, appeared in Fuerstenberg. He was born as the only son of the music conductor at the court of King Stanislaus in Luneville in 1747 and had attended the monastery school there. He then came to Sèvres as a floral painter, went from there to Niderviller, and had worked in all existing factories until he arrived in Muenster, Westphalia, completely destitute. As he said, he was able to subsist only by painting ornaments on ladies' dresses and accessories. Before he arrived in Braunschweig, he had been compelled to sell his watch in Hanover. Since his experience was considerable, he was kept on in Fuerstenberg, and he earned the title *Fuerstlicher Intendant* (Administrative Officer to the Prince). He was a reformer who instituted changes that helped to stabilize conditions during the nineteenth century. The factory is still operating in the old Fuerstenberg Castle where it had its beginnings over 200 years ago.

Berlin

Frederick the Great was called the Soldier King, but he was also a passionate admirer of porcelain, although the two—war and porcelain—would seem to be quite inimical. He made every effort to establish a porcelain factory in his own country. He almost succeeded at the end of the Second Silesian War, when he had the Meissen factory dismantled and its workers deported to Berlin. However, the peace agreement at Hubertsburg hampered his ambitions. In 1751 the wealthy wool manufacturer Wilhelm Kaspar Wegeli offered Frederick his services in establishing a hard porcelain factory in Berlin.

Wegeli received a building and some land from the King and started his factory there. His friendly relations with the director of the Hoechst porcelain factory assured him a supply of paste and the correct design for the construction of the kiln.

Frederick the Great had occupied Meissen in the course of the Seven Years' War, and Wegeli had had an opportunity to thoroughly inspect the factory. Not much is known about the men who worked for Wegeli. The arcanist Niklaus Paul came from Hoechst, the sculptor Ernst Heinrich Reichart formed the models, and the miniature-painter Isaac Clauce (he had studied with miniature-painter Wolfgang in Berlin) came in 1753, went to Meissen, but later returned to Berlin. He was a first-rate figure painter. We know of a few figures by the sculptor Reichart. A Pair of Lovers (Fig. 38) is the most outstanding.

As early as 1757, Wegeli closed his factory again. Reichart, who had learned the arcanum from Niklaus Paul, continued on his own until 1761 when the Berlin merchant Gotzkowski purchased the factory and its stock for 3,000 thalers and the arcanum for 4,000 thalers. Niklaus Paul had gone to Fuerstenberg. This expert on soils and clays is probably the most interesting of the many wandering figures of the eighteenth century. He had no patience to stay anywhere for long. From Fuerstenberg he went to Hoexter and on to Weesp, as previously noted.

Frederick promised to raise enough money to keep the factory going. When the existence of the factory seemed assured, Reichart relinquished his plans to move to Gotha, and in return he received rent-free lodgings, wood for fuel, and one hundred thalers a year. With Reichart, Gotzkowski also took over the painter Clauce. The Saxon *Kommerzienrat* (Councilor of Commerce) Grieninger was appointed director. Two more workers arrived from Meissen, one of them Elias Meyer, to whom Berlin owes its best figures. He had received his training from Kaendler. In 1762 Gotzkowski already employed 150 workers and 150 apprentices, who were trained as painters and sculptors. Other artists arrived from Meissen: the master painter Carl Wilhelm Boehme, who had been painting landscapes and figures for twenty-five years; Johann Baltasar Borrmann, painter of battle scenes and figures; and Carl Jakob Klipfel, floral and mosaic painter. The molders Mueller, Kuehnel, Bergmann, and the painters Lohse, Toscani, Horn, and Buettner deserted Meissen as well. We meet Toscani again in 1765, as a skilled figure painter in Fuerstenberg. Joachim Duwald became kiln master and constructed the best kilns. Riedel and Meerheim, both from Meissen, worked on the colors.

In spite of this first-class staff of artists Gotzkowski was not able to keep the factory going. The workers had not been paid since 1763, and he had invested too much money in the physical plant of the factory. He offered it to the King for 225,000 thalers, and Frederick accepted his offer. Gotzkowski had made an excellent deal. From then on the Berlin porcelain factory was managed under the royal account. Before the mayor and his council Gotzkowski had to declare under oath that he had disclosed to the King "all the secrets and sciences, the art and all manipulations" on which the factory was founded. He had not held back any important information, nor given away secrets to a third party.

The King invested 200,000 thalers in additional equipment and visited the factory in person on September 11, 1763, spending more than two hours on the premises. New buildings, a new vault for preparing the porcelain paste, and new kilns were under construction. Grieninger was still director. In 1770 the staff consisted of 500 persons, and the orphanage of Potsdam supplied the apprentices. In the soil near Potsdam, kaolin was discovered, and the factory processed 15,000 hundredweight a year. Of all factories Berlin paid the best salaries. Master modeler Meyer earned 2,000 thalers, as did the superintendent of the painting studio, Clauce. Director Grieninger made 1,400 thalers. The lowest wages, sixty thalers, were earned by the night watchman. As Berlin's mark the King selected a scepter in underglaze blue. He himself was one of the fac-

Fig. 38. Pair of Lovers with Bird Cage. Berlin, period of Wegeli, around 1755. Model by Heinrich Reichart

tory's best customers. His gifts were dispatched all over the world, particularly to Catherine of Russia. In 1763 he had ordered a large dinner service for his new palace. From time to time he paid a *douceur* (bonus) for exceptionally good work, frequently as much as fifty thalers. No women and children worked in the factory, but the men often had to work twelve hours a day or eighty-four hours a week. Berlin bought foreign porcelain, too, above all from Meissen and Sèvres. Sèvres did not manufacture true porcelain, but the exquisite painting on its soft-paste porcelain made up for this.

Visitors from every country and from every strata of society came to Berlin and Grieninger took pride

Fig. 39. Plate and tureen with lid from the Royal service for Sanssouci. Berlin, 1769–1770

in showing them around. The King spent over 200,000 thalers on his own requirements over a period of twenty years. The arcanist Reichart died in 1764 of the wasting disease, as tuberculosis was called at the time. The chemist Kretzmar took his place. The products of the Berlin factory were intended for persons of wealth, as were those of Ludwigsburg, Frankenthal, Nymphenburg, and Meissen. The porcelain from the Thuringia Woods could be afforded by those of more modest means.

Berlin established branches in other cities to distribute its wares. Each buyer had to pay for half of his account in gold, and the other half was entered as credit.

The small tureen shown in Figure 39 was part of the service which the King had ordered for his Sanssouci Palace. It was made for the Japanese Palace, which was equipped with a Chinese kitchen. The border of the saucer is done in openwork and the polychrome painting with chinoiserie is patterned after Pillement and Boucher. This kind of table service consisted of 140 individual pieces. It was possible to buy these settings in twenty-seven variations, and the prices ranged according to the quality of decoration:

Without ornament (plain) medium quality	196 florins
With natural flowers	375 florins
With birds	881 florins

The most expensive decoration—with *dessin* and birds—cost 1,174 florins.

The two master modelers—the best of twelve modelers—were Friedrich Elias Meyer and his brother Wilhelm Christian Meyer, experienced craftsmen who had an artistic style of their own. Elias Meyer had worked in Meissen since July 1, 1748; he had been highly respected and had received a salary of thirty-eight thalers a month. However, in Meissen he had worked in the shadow of Kaendler, and here in Berlin he was able to create his own models. His favorite subjects were mythological and allegorical. Many of his figures are representations of the gods of antiquity, of the five senses, of air, water, earth, fire, etc. One group (Fig. 40), an allegorical presentation of Vanity, belongs to his late period and is unpainted. Wilhelm Christian was a sculptor and later the rector of the Academy of Fine Arts. He worked in the factory after 1766.

Fig. 40. Allegorical group representing Vanity. Berlin 1770. Model by Elias Meyer

Many changes took place in the factory after the death of Frederick the Great on August 17, 1786. In a letter, Director Grieninger gives a vivid description of the sense of loss and sorrow that prevailed in Berlin: "My God, what gloomy silence. Everywhere nothing but sighs and tears. And the sight of so many graying brave soldiers, crying for their beloved Frederick, under whose command they won so many victories. Never has a King been mourned so woefully by his army and his people. He was the only one."

A commission including Grieninger and the painter Klipfel determined the changes that were to be effected in the porcelain factory. The industrialization of the nineteenth century brought with it several innovations. New coal-burning kilns were constructed. A new era was ushered in by new designs and new forms. The factory is still operating successfully today, having survived two World Wars.

Frankenthal

The history of the Frankenthal factory spans forty-five years. The most important events were:

1755 Founded and equipped in the vacant armory in Frankenthal by Karl Hannong of Strassburg.
1755 November. First successful firing. Master modeler Johann Lanz of Strassburg.
1756 Elector Karl Theodor and his wife visit the factory.
1757 Arrival of workers from Meissen and Hoechst.
1757 Death of Karl Hannong; management is passed on to his grandson, Joseph Adam Hannong.
1757–1764
Johann Friedrich Lueck, master modeler.
1759 Paul Hannong sells factory to his son, Joseph Adam Hannong.
1761 Setbacks in business.
1762 Karl Theodor, Elector of the Pfalz, buys the factory for 40,000 florins and pays 1,000 florins for the arcanum.

Fig. 41. Plate from service for the Electress Elisabeth Augusta. Frankenthal around 1759

1762–1770
Most productive period. Adam Bergdoll of Hoechst, Director.
1767 Karl Gottlieb Lueck, master modeler.
1770 Technical director Simon Feilner assisting Bergdoll.
1774 Discovery of kaolin in local soil; mixed with clay from Passau.
1775 The factory employs five clerks, twenty-three painters, twelve turners, seven repairers, three glazers, five grinders, five laborers. Altogether sixty persons.
1775 Adam Bauer, master modeler.
1779 Peter Melchior from Hoechst, master modeler.
1788 Beginning of decline.
1793 Michael Offenstein, master modeler.
1794 Frankenthal occupied by the French; leased to van Recum.
1800 Production is suspended.

A few figures should be added to this short summary. Frankenthal's total production in 1794 shows an inventory of 200 groups, 600 figures, and 500 small porcelain objects, not counting the tableware.

In 1748 Hannong had obtained a vague description of the production of porcelain from two workers from Hoechst and Meissen, Johann Gottlieb Rothe and Christian Wilhelm Loewenfinck. However, both were not capable of manufacturing hard porcelain. To get results, Joseph Jakob Ringler had to move to Strassburg from Hoechst in 1752. He knew how to construct the kiln and mix the correct paste. However, since Hannong was not permitted to produce porcelain with polychrome and gold decoration, and since Sèvres held a state monopoly in France, he moved to Frankenthal in Alsace. At this time, Alsace was considered a foreign province, not an integral part of the French state.

The factory was one of the most successful of the eighteenth century, as far as the production of tableware and figures was concerned. The master modelers were mostly sculptors who also worked on monuments. We know of the following:

Johann Lanz (1755–1761)
Johann Friedrich Lueck (1758–1764)
Franz Konrad Linck (1762–1766)
Johann Peter Melchior (1779–1796)
Adam Bauer (1777–1778)

The painters, too, did outstanding work, espe-

Fig. 42. Pair of Lovers representing Spring. Frankenthal before 1755. Model by Johann Wilhelm Lanz

cially Johann Bernhard Magnus, Jakob Osterspey, and Winterstein. Through the years, fifty-five painters worked at Frankenthal. We have already mentioned Andreas Philipp Oettner, Gottlieb Friedrich Riedel, Johann Gottlieb Rothe, Franz Josef Weber, Friedrich Weissbrod, and Winterstein. The pictured plate (Fig. 41) from the service for the Elector's wife, Elisabeth Augusta, was probably painted by one of the first three painters named above. The flowers are painted in one color only, in *camaieu* purple, and the monogram "EA" is in gold. The variations and combinations of this flower design are limitless, ranging from modest scattered blossoms, which served to hide defects in the glaze, to the majestic rose, a true

Fig. 43. Pair of Lovers representing Autumn. Frankenthal before 1755. Model by Lanz

testimony of the superior skill of a talented floral painter.

The shapes of Frankenthal's ware were unusually ornate, almost as ornate as Meissen's. Every demand and whim of the royal household had to be satisfied: mirror frames, cane handles, barber bowls, ewers, breakfast sets and cups without handles—so-called *Koppchen*—vases of all shapes, table clocks and wall clocks, salt shakers, wine coolers, tureens in the shape of swans or turkeys, chess figures, flasks for smelling salts, candelabras with two or more arms, centerpieces, and tableaus for hanging—but also plain in-

Fig. 44. "The Child's Birthday." Frankenthal 1773. Model by Karl Gottlieb Lueck

expensive plates. All this was for sale, either in white or with colorful decorations. The price was determined by the quality of painting.

In London, at the Victoria and Albert Museum, there is a plate from Frankenthal, painted and signed by Feilner, with sixty small bouquets, in sixty different colors. Each painter had his specialty. Winterstein, for instance, only painted children, Indian figures, and figures from classical mythology. Magnus specialized in children, landscapes, and figures taken from Watteau; Osterspey in figures from mythology, children, and landscapes; Arnold in figures, pastoral scenes, and birds; Herold in medallions with Imperial portraits—and so on. In this way, each painter became thoroughly versed in his own particular field. Since all of them worked from models, there must have been a rich variety of engravings to copy from.

The figures and groups were more outstanding than the tableware. After 1755, Johann Lanz from Strassburg was the master modeler. In church records he is referred to as the "sculptor of the factory" whenever he is mentioned as godfather or as witness to a marriage. His allegorical group representing spring (Fig. 42) is striking for its vitality and is reminiscent of his Strassburg faiences. The contrast between the maid's wide-open eyes and the half-closed eyes of the bagpipe player serves to differentiate the two rustic figures. The flower basket and the bouquet at the maid's neckline establish the representation of spring. Two further allegories, one of autumn and one of winter, also feature these two figures, which were modeled after engravings by Amiconi.

Lanz placed another pair of lovers, representing autumn, in a vine-clad arbor (Fig. 43). He filled the basket with grapes instead of flowers. The factory's price list published in 1760 in the *Journal des Commerce* contains the following description: "Love Inspired by Wine." This pair cost ninety-six florins with the arbor and sixty-six florins without.

Johann Friedrich Lueck was a modeler during the same period as Lanz. Lueck was the son of a sculptor from Saxony and was born in Freiburg in 1727. He learned repairing as a fourteen-year-old boy in Meissen. After running away from Meissen in 1757, he came to Frankenthal via Hoechst. "His costumed figures impress us first as somewhat stiff and conventional, but we soon overlook this shortcoming because the modeling displays an amiable freshness, imaginative design and graceful elegance." When he received his "Letter of Pardon" from Meissen, he returned there in 1764.

His older brother, Karl Gottlieb Lueck, also from Meissen, came to Frankenthal, also via Hoechst, in 1758. In the church records he is referred to as "artistic repairer of the local porcelain factory," and in the personnel roster he is called *Poussierer*. He was the father of nine children, and at the time of his death, the youngest was not yet of age but had already learned the repairing trade in the factory. The group entitled "The Child's Birthday" (Fig. 44) was repaired by him. The characters are purely costume figures but are very appealing.

The famous sculptor Konrad Linck worked in the factory for a short time. He was Electoral *statuarius*. To this day, a street in Frankenthal bears his name; he obviously was a famous man. We know Johann Peter Melchior and Adam Bauer of Ludwigsburg. The latter had left Ludwigsburg because of mounting debts and had established residence in Mannheim with the intention of seeking employment as master modeler in Frankenthal. Apparently his models were not appreciated. The Elector was not pleased with his modest groups of figures, and Bauer was dismissed after one year.

Frankenthal closed its factory in 1799 and tried to dispose of the merchandise by auction. The new era despised the fanciful small porcelain marvels, and the ornate curves of the rococo were replaced by a cool and straight design. However, much that bears witness to this lighthearted and spirited time has been preserved in museums and private collections.

Ludwigsburg

On April 5, 1758, Duke Carl Eugen von Wuerttemburg, a spendthrift and splendor-loving monarch, decided to acquire a new jewel for his crown: a porcelain factory. Five months later he engaged, as arcanist and director, the expert Joseph Jakob Ringler, who is well known to us by now. Ringler remained in the Duke's service for forty-five years up to his death. He earned seventy-five florins a month and free lodgings. He sold the Duke his well-guarded secret for one hundred ducats.

Within the same year, eighteen craftsmen arrived in Ludwigsburg, among them the repairer and modeler Johann Hoez and Joseph Nees. The latter we shall meet again in Zurich. Also making an appearance were Johann Carl Vogelmann and the world-famous painter, draftsman, and engraver Gottlieb Friedrich Riedel, who had painted in Meissen, Hoechst, and Frankenthal previously. I shall go into more detail about some of these men, but most of them had one thing in common: they wandered from place to place dreaming of better wages.

Fig. 45. Vase with perforated lid, so-called *brûle parfum*. Ludwigsburg around 1765. Painted by Riedel. Height 1 ft. 10 in. (57.5 cm)

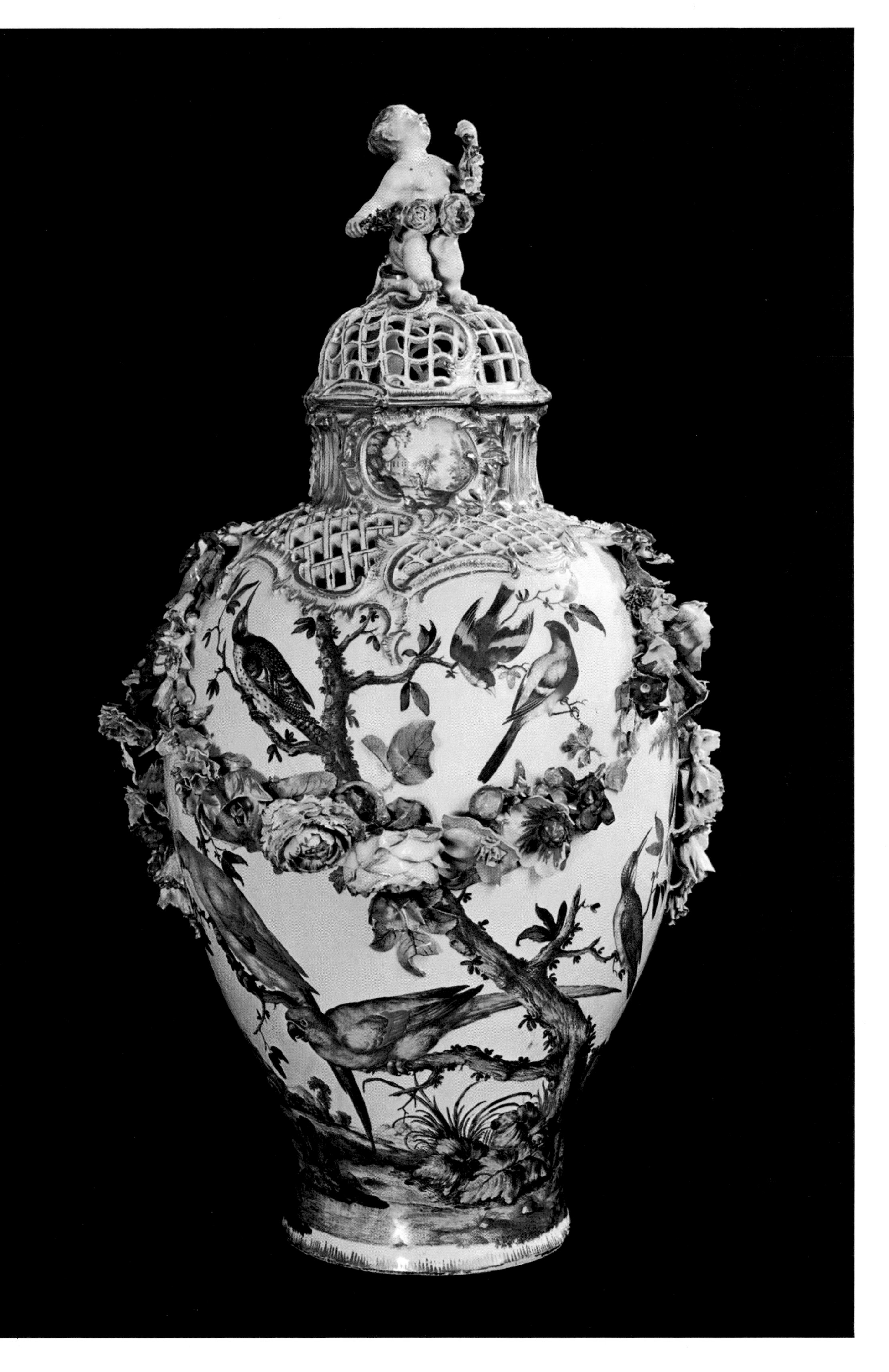

The "Manufactory of true porcelain" was established in an old gamekeeper's house in the Schorndorfstrasse at an expense of 4,000 ducats. The porcelain clay was bought from the well-known quarries in Passau and was mixed with local clay from Hornberg. The salaries for the workmen totaled 16,000 florins. One half of this sum was paid out in cash, and they had to take the other half in form of porcelain seconds which they were permitted to sell to the peasants and less affluent citizens.

The number of workmen employed was highest in 1766, when the staff consisted of 154 people. The polychrome painters and repairers were highest in the hierarchy, that is, they were regarded as most valuable to the factory and were paid accordingly. During the same year, the factory employed twenty-three painters with fourteen apprentices, eleven turners with fifteen apprentices, two formers with sixteen apprentices, and eight men who worked at the kilns. Riedel was chief painter from 1759 to 1779, and Johann Ignaz Stegmann was master turner. Bonaventura Walcher, the kiln master, was Ringler's brother-in-law from Munich, and he and Ringler together supervised the kilns and the firing. There was an average of twenty firings per year. Ludwigsburg's best years were 1760–1770. In 1760 a faience factory was added to the porcelain factory. It worked under the supervision of Adam Friedrich von Loewenfinck's widow, who had married a Major de Becke. Success and misfortune alternated as in all other factories. In 1771, the Duke decided that the factory could maintain itself without subsidy from him, but in 1776 he again advanced additional funds. When he died in 1793, all subsidies came to an end. After a short period of recovery, when the new Louis XVI style became the vogue, King William I decided to liquidate the factory.

Fig. 46. Satirical group: "Gentleman with the Oversized Bow." Ludwigsburg around 1765. Model by Nees

Artists who worked in Ludwigsburg but left after a short time hoping to find a more lucrative place of employment included:

Gottlieb Friedrich Riedel, born 1724, pupil of the Saxon court painter Sylvestre; in Meissen from 1743 to 1756; in Hoechst in 1757, from whence he went to Paris and Frankenthal in the same year. He painted in Ludwigsburg from 1759 to 1779, then worked as a copper engraver in Augsburg, where he died in 1784.

Andreas Philipp Ettner, painter in Vienna around 1755; 1756, one year in Nymphenburg; 1759, in Frankenthal, traveled to Ludwigsburg in the same year; 1765–1767, in Hoechst; dismissed because he was dissatisfied with the piecemeal payments. There is a painter called Oettner in Vienna again in 1785.

Johann Philipp Dannhoefer, whom we have encountered in various places before, was in Ludwigsburg from 1762 to 1790.

Franz Joseph Weber painted miniatures in Ludwigsburg in the early 1760s then went to Kelsterbach; 1769–1770, in Frankenthal; then in Hoechst as director and arcanist; 1798, in Ilmenau; author of the famous *Die Kunst, das aechte Porzellan zu verfertigen (The Art of Producing True Porcelain)*, Hanover, 1798.

Johann Philipp Bechel, born 1726. He was twenty years old when as a blue-glaze painter he came to Hoechst from Fulda, where he was one of the first workers. Christian Wilhelm Loewenfinck taught him

Fig. 47. Fair booths. Ludwigsburg around 1765. Model by Joseph Nees

polychrome painting; he went to Ludwigsburg in 1759, but in 1771 his name appears again on the list of workers in Hoechst. He stayed there until the factory closed.

These men were quality painters who changed their places of employment frequently. All of them, and equally their new employers, took great risks in the expectation of having their aspirations fulfilled.

Ludwigsburg, like all other porcelain factories of the day, manufactured tableware and figures. The splendor of Carl Eugen's royal household demanded tableware produced in his own factory. It never equalled the pure white of Meissen's and the paste remained a dirty gray all through the manufacturing process. However, the shapes and decoration could stand up to any competition. Occasionally, there were true masterpieces, such as the service for the Duke's friend Marchesa Giovanelli-Martinengo of Venice, or the splendid vases which in all likelihood were designed and painted by Riedel (Fig. 45).

Riedel's pieces were designed entirely in the rococo manner. He developed his own very special Ludwigsburg style, which is distinguished by its beauty and elegance from all other products of the second half of the eighteenth century. In his works we find borders modeled in relief, *Schuppenmuster*

Fig. 48. Pair of Lovers. Ludwigsburg around 1765. Model by J. Ch. Haselmeier

(scale design) which covers the whole body of the vase, leaving just enough space for the decoration, vases with molded flower wreaths and trellises woven through with acanthus leaves, and laurel wreaths and ribbons. The graphics collection in the Wuerttemberg National Gallery has many sketches drawn by Riedel for the factory.

The loveliest bouquets of flowers were painted by Johann Friedrich Kirschner of Bayreuth, who was one of the Ludwigsburg painters for five years, from 1770 to 1775. Johann Friedrich Steinkopf specialized in landscapes and animals, but the best painter of birds was Riedel. Every kind of decoration was done by first-rate artists who saw to it that every

Fig. 49. Playful Bacchanti. Ludwigsburg around 1760–1765. Model by Joh. Ch. Wilhelm Beyer

dish was executed with great taste. Ludwigsburg was famous not only for its tableware; the figure modelers did equally fine work.

One of Ludwigsburg's first treasures was a centerpiece for a table measuring seventeen feet in length and eleven feet in width. A basin held Neptune standing in a chariot drawn by sea horses amid grottoes with tritons, naiads, dolphins, and children with fishes—a colossal work and a technical triumph which did honor to the new factory. Johann Carl Vogelmann modeled the first figures. The first repairers came to Ludwigsburg with him: the sculptor Goetz and the deaf mute Joseph Nees. They each received the same wages, twenty-six florins.

Nees stayed in Ludwigsburg from 1759 to 1767. He later went to Zurich via Kuenersburg and Ellwangen.

In addition to a series of dancers, Nees may have modeled the Stalls at the Fair (Fig. 47) and the small satirical scene of the Gentleman with the Oversized Bow. (Fig. 46) The gentleman steps through the archway and has to be assisted by another to make certain that his oversized bow will not get crushed. He is ridiculed by one figure in the foreground. The peacock in the background symbolizes mockery directed against the wearer of the bow.

Jean Jacques Louis was fifty-nine years old when he replaced Goetz in 1762. He remained in Ludwigsburg as master repairer and master modeler until his death in 1772. Having worked in Tournai before, in 1754, and from 1756 to 1760 in the French factories of Sceaux, Strassburg and Orléans, he was an experienced artist when he came to Ludwigsburg. To recognize the work he did at Ludwigsburg, one must be acquainted with what he produced at his former places of employment, particularly at Tournai. While there, he signed a large parrot with an *L*.

Johann Christof Haselmeier was an accomplished modeler. He started out as a wax repairer and was a student of François Lejeune around 1760. Lejeune was the Duke's *premier sculpteur* and professor at the art academy. A large pair of lovers (Fig. 48), attributed to Haselmeier, still shows the influence of Lejeune.

The most famous of the Ludwigsburg modelers was Johann Christian Wilhelm Beyer. The Duke granted him an excellent education. He was sent to Paris at the age of twenty-two to study architecture, and from there he went to Rome where he studied painting and sculpture. After supervising the repairers at the porcelain factory from 1759 to 1767, he moved to Vienna, where together with other sculptors he created the statues in the park at Schoenbrunn. His work at the factory was influenced by classical sculpture. Some illustrations of his figures are included in his *Oesterreichische Merkwuerdigkeiten die Bild- und Baukunst betreffen" (Austrian Phenomena Regarding Art and Architecture*) published in Vienna in 1779. Two of his most important works are a playful bacchantic group (Fig. 49) and a series of musicians, including a trumpeter (Fig. 50). A good part of the sculpture and painted ornaments in the new castle in Stuttgart (now destroyed) is also attributed to him. "He succeeded to a remarkable degree in blending the classic and French influence and to achieve a perfect union between the austere dignity of classic art and the vitality of his own era" (Pfeiffer).

Other modelers included Joseph Weinmueller, Adam Bauer, and Valtin Sonnenschein, whom we shall meet again in Zurich. Bauer was Lejeune's pupil in 1758, became court modeler in 1772, and after 1774 was professor of sculpture at the Solitude. He fled to France in 1777, and after 1780 he worked with Beyer in Vienna. The groups and figures which are today displayed in Schloss Ludwigsburg are excellent examples of the work of these artists.

Neudeck-Nymphenburg

It was regarded as "a necessary attribute to the splendor and dignity of an aristocratic court" to own a real porcelain factory. We have met two imposters who pretended to know how to produce true porcelain: Loewenfinck in Hoechst and Glaser in Fuerstenberg. In Neudeck near Munich the same drama repeated itself. The potter Franz Ignaz Niedermayer, supposedly a man with experience in the field, had in 1747 promised Elector Maximilian III Joseph that he would build a porcelain factory for him. A worker from Meissen allegedly had disclosed the arcanum to him "while they were enjoying some wine together and exchanging confidences." He would get a supply of clay from Philipp Stallmeier in Hafnerzell.

On January 20, 1745, the Elector had married Maria Anna Sophie, the daughter of Friedrich August II, Elector of Saxony and King of Poland. It would give him much pleasure to present his young wife with a porcelain factory. Since Niedermayer's work would not produce any satisfactory results, the painter Jakob Helchis from Vienna was called, and also the repairer Schreiber and the kiln master Lippis. The small Castle Neudeck was put at their disposal. The Elector had inherited thirty-five million in debts, and money came in at a mere trickle, but the workmen were paid. However, when it became obvious that the Viennese could not manufacture

Fig. 50. Trumpeter from the group of solo musicians. Ludwigsburg around 1760–1765. Model by Joh. Ch. Wilhelm Beyer

porcelain either, even though the castle was well equipped and both kilns were burning well, the Elector withheld further funds in 1750 and dismissed them. The building was again given over, free of charge, to the potter Niedermayer.

When Count Sigmund von Haimhausen, an excellent businessman, arrived in Munich, Neudeck came to life again. During the summer of 1753, a man whom we have come to know very well appeared in Munich: Joseph Jakob Ringler from Vienna, who had sold his arcanum to Hoechst three years before, and again to Strassburg in 1752. "It is common knowledge all over the world that Ringler was an expert in the construction of kilns and knew

Fig. 51. Tureen with saucer. Nymphenburg 1755. Probably painted by Andreas Oettner

the correct formula to produce hard-paste porcelain," wrote Franz Joseph Weber in his first book on porcelain, which was published in 1798. Ringler remained in Neudeck until January 30, 1757, when he moved on to Memmingen. But these years were enough to enable Nymphenburg to manufacture the finest porcelain that came out of the second half of the eighteenth century. As arcanist and kiln master, Ringler was paid five florins a week, an additional three florins for the preparation of the paste and three florins more for each firing. He was not willing to part with his arcanum, but there was no need for this any longer. The chemist Johann Paul Haertl had carefully listened to Ringler's instructions and had made note of everything he saw and heard. He was capable of keeping the production going.

The staff consisted of capable experts. In 1755 thirty men were employed in Neudeck. Franz Anton Bustelli arrived to work as a modeler on November 3, 1754. Andreas Oettner was chief painter and was succeeded by Georg Christoph Lindenmann, whose landscape on a covered tureen (Fig. 51), dating from around 1755, clearly shows Meissen's influence. These tureens were precious objects and occasionally cost as much as one hundred florins. They were modeled by Franz Anton Bustelli between 1755 and 1760.

After Lindenmann's departure in 1760, the painter Cajetan Putscher was hired to paint landscapes, figures, and animal scenes. There were as many as fifty firings in Neudeck in 1757, and the value of the porcelain production was estimated at 27,100 florins.

A few words about Bustelli: In older books he is referred to as a *Tessiner* (a native of the Swiss canton of Tessin) from Intragna, since a Casa Bustelli is standing there to this day. However, later research by the curator of the *Bayrisches Nationalmuseum* in Munich casts doubt on the assumption that he actually came from Tessin. During the seventeenth century the name Bustelli had already appeared in Bavaria.

Next to Kaendler and Melchior he is one of the greatest porcelain artists of the eighteenth century. There is an irresistibly graceful charm in his figures, especially his Italian comedians (Fig. 52). This group represents eight ladies and an equal number of gentlemen dressed in the *Commedia dell'Arte's* traditional costumes of the period; the characters include Capitano, Arlecchino, Octavio, Dottore, Isabella, and others. Compared with other porcelain figures of this period, it cannot be denied that Bustelli is Kaendler's equal, although unlike Kaendler he is not a master of the baroque but a true artist of the rococo. Bustelli worked in Neudeck and later in Nymphenburg until his death in 1763.

There were other modelers who worked with Bustelli, less outstanding artists known only by their names. The repairers and turners were numerous. One notable repairer was Franz Josef Aest, who had previously worked in Hoechst and Ludwigsburg. Peter Anton Seefried and Adam Clair were well known as well.

In 1761, when the space in Neudeck became unbearably cramped, the factory was moved to Schloss Nymphenburg, where it is still in operation in the same historic premises. The value of the sales inventory then stood at 54,200 florins. Haertl stayed on as arcanist and manager, although he is not mentioned in the list of officials. He suffered the fate of most arcanists—that is, he became dispensable when the factory's production proceeded smoothly. "And so it happened that Haertl suddenly fell into disgrace. The factory owed its undreamed of progress to him alone. But the politics of ruthless ingratitude had sacrificed Niedermayer and Ringler within a short period of time. It now claimed its third victim," wrote Friedrich Hofmann in his book on Nymphenburg.

Fig. 52. Isabella from the *Commedia dell'Arte.* Nymphenburg, 1755–1760. Model by Franz Anton Bustelli

Fig. 53. Platter from the Electoral service. Nymphenburg around 1755

During the year 1765, there were 187 persons employed in Nymphenburg: twenty-four polychrome and blue painters, sixty-five apprentice painters, including the color mixers and gold polishers, one master modeler, seventy-five repairers, turners, and workmen attending to the kilns. Few other factories had as many expert craftsmen. The salaries totaled 21,000 florins. Twenty-eight thousand florins were entered as profit. A large bowl with a colorful bouquet of flowers (Fig. 53), ordered for the Electoral court in Munich, dates from this period. Its flowers may have been painted by the miniature-painter Josef Weiss.

The year 1766 saw the first fiasco. Several porcelain factories had opened in France and Germany around the middle of the eighteenth century, and this contributed to a general decline. If the Duke's coffers had not made up the deficit from time to time, the whole enterprise would have gone bankrupt. Conditions for trade in Bavaria were poor. The Elector decreed that production should be reduced. The golden age was over. Even Count Haimhausen retired from the directorship of the factory. The master modeler Dominicus Auliczek, who had been engaged after Bustelli's death, demonstrated much good will and was made inspector of the factory, an office he held until 1793. The finance commission drew up extensive instructions for him consisting of thirty-two points. All expenses concerning the workmen and wood and coal used as fuel had to be paid out of the factory's income.

Nymphenburg specialized in the so-called *Tuerkenkoppchen* (cups without handles), which were exported to Turkey. In 1774 Wertheimer in Vienna bought 3,400 dozen of these *Koppchen,* a pair of which cost only 12 xr in white.

Maximilian III Joseph died on December 30, 1777. His successor was Karl Theodor, Elector of the Palatinate, who preferred the products of his own factory in Frankenthal. He opened a branch of Frankenthal porcelain in Munich. In the year 1782, only twenty-eight porcelain workers were employed in Nymphenburg. Despite all difficulties, the management had succeeded in paying off a debt of 22,000 florins, and the inventory contained porcelain worth 100,000 florins. In recognition Aulizcek received the title of *Wirklicher jedoch nicht frequentierender Hofkammerrat* (Court Chamberlain without attending Privileges).

In 1783 and 1785 business was so poor that there was not enough money to order raw materials. Conditions became so critical that it was almost impossible to continue. Power struggles, envy, and conceit had done their share to create more and more tensions among the workers. Because of his advanced age, Haimhausen retired in 1788. Since then the factory has survived two centuries in spite of all difficulties. The porcelain now is modern, but the traditional old models of the lovely comedians still form part of the production.

The Small German Factories

ANSBACH-BRUCKBERG

On May 20, 1768, in Bruckberg, the porcelain painters Dortu, Gerlach, Stenglein, and Telorac and the repairers Bartholome and Koehler had imbibed three measures of brandy and thirty-eight measures of beer and had to be carried home by their apprentices. There is a report in the state archives in Nuremberg which relates this idyllic little incident. A tendency to go beyond decent limits when quenching their thirst was shared by many porcelain workers. The crowding together of many men of very diverse intellectual development easily led to excesses, but these were severely punished by the management. Complaints from the village inhabitants about noise, drunkenness, thefts, and brawls were commonplace.

Ansbach was founded by the twenty-one-year-old Margrave Alexander. On his travels and during visits to the palaces of his friends, he had admired the beautiful porcelain, and it was his ambition to become the owner of a porcelain factory. His table was set with dinnerware from the Ansbach faience factory, which had been in existence since 1710 and where the famous exile from Meissen, Adam Friedrich von Loewenfinck, worked in 1737. After the invention of true porcelain, faience was regarded as extremely dated. The most insignificant little monarch felt that he should eat from his own factory's porcelain, and that he should be in a position to present it as a gift to his equals.

It appears that there was considerable demand for Meissen porcelain in the vicinity of Ansbach. The Saxon porcelain merchant Lippmann repeatedly advertised in the Ansbach newspapers that he had "again brought to Ansbach a collection of tea and coffee services of Dresden porcelain and all kinds of figures."

Alexander was the offspring of the Hohenzollern family in Franconia. Concern for his subjects seems to have been one of his considerations when he founded his porcelain factory. "One can rejoice when such a factory succeeds in feeding a number of diligent people and in bringing some money into the country . . ." the Margrave wrote. In 1757 and 1758 a few craftsmen came to Ansbach who appeared to have some knowledge of the arcanum. During that period, as previously noted, Frederick the Great's occupation made conditions in Meissen precarious, and several workmen looked for employment elsewhere. Johann Friedrich Kaendler, Johann Carl Gerlach, Carl Gottlieb Laut, and Johann Christian Plinior all moved from Meissen to Bruckberg. Kaendler, a nephew of the great master from Meissen, brought the formulas for the composition of paste and colors. The painter Gerlach, a Catholic, left Protestant Ansbach in 1758 but returned again in 1762. He had worked as a miniature-painter for Wegeli in Berlin, and he took models and colors with him to Ansbach. This may explain perhaps why the first Ansbach figures resembled Berlin models.

Aside from Kaendler, two other modelers were known for their tableware and figures: Carl Gottlieb Laut from Saxony, who was only seventeen years old; and Johann Friedrich Scherber, whose background is unknown. Laut was master modeler, and his style was quite typical. His figures' eyes are half closed, they are painted in a reddish hue, and they have claw-like fingers and an oversized figure. Karl Ludwig Bartholome was a repairer and assembled the individual parts of the figures. Since he too was a Catholic, he went to Fulda in 1770.

These painters and modelers used apprentices from Ansbach's surroundings—for instance, the son of the barber Schoellhammer. Schoellhammer worked very successfully in Ansbach for forty years, first as a painter and then as superintendent of the painting department. It was probably Schoellhammer who painted a tankard (Fig. 54) after an engraving by Johann Elias Nilson of Augsburg.

The excellent quality of the decorations contributed much to Ansbach's fame. Every piece produced by this factory was painted with much care, and it can be stated without exaggeration that few small factories achieved such excellent results. A newspaper advertisement of October 20, 1762 informs us that the merchandise offered by Ansbach included, besides coffee sets, candelabras, butter dishes, small baskets, *Chacan* (cane handles), tobacco boxes, *Devisen* (small allegorical figures used as table decorations, holding small notes in their hands), sword handles, snuff boxes, flasks for smelling salts, and all kinds of figures.

Italian comedians were still much in demand around the middle of the eighteenth century, and Ansbach had its own Harlequin with his partner Columbine, and also its Pantalone, Pierrot, and Scapin. There was another favorite group which was modeled after Ferriol's work, *Recueil de Cent*

Fig. 54. Tankard. Ansbach around 1760. Painted by Johann Melchior Schoellhammer after an engraving by Nilson

Estamps représentant différent Nations du Levant (Collection of One Hundred Prints Representing Different Nations of the Levant). The modeler Laut copied his lovely Turkish and Oriental figures from this book. Ansbach also created the large Pair of Lovers shown here (Fig. 55) and several putti and street criers. These were typical of the models by Bartholome. As he left Ansbach again in 1770, we can date his figures of children. Some he also signed with a *B*.

What did these figures cost? A large figure like Figure 55 cost twenty-four florins, smaller figures went for eight florins, very small figures were priced at three florins. Everybody's taste could be satisfied in Ansbach, according to one's ability to pay.

When funds ran low, Ansbach also disposed of its merchandise by means of lotteries, even if this meant the risk of a certain loss. The lotteries always raised a few hundred guilders. Such lotteries were held in 1767, 1770, and 1793. In most cases 6,000 lottery tickets were printed and sold at 2 florins 48 xr each. The first prizes were always complete tea or coffee sets with either monochrome or polychrome decoration. The first prize was valued at 600 florins, the smallest prize at 1 florin 30 xr, and at times one half of the prize's value was paid in cash. All tickets were sold for the first lottery, but no longer for the subsequent ones.

A great change took place after 1780, and the rococo style was superseded by the neo-classical. The artist Stenglein, who came from Paris and Ludwigsburg, was famous for this later style in Ansbach. He painted with one color only, mainly in purple. The court scenes were outdated. The new style raised the factory's income: 4,730 florins in 1776, 8,700 florins in 1780, and three years later, 12,340 florins. Most of the merchandise was sold to Holland and Turkey. The Turkish merchant Benevist had bought 70,000 *Tuerkenbecher* (cups without handles) in 1784, but they had to be marked with the Meissen swords. There were very favorable contemporary comments about the factory. Baron von Bibra wrote to a friend: "I can assure you, my dear friend, that I was so well pleased with the equipment and workmanship I found in this factory which contributes so greatly to Ansbach's benefit and honor, that the difficult journey I had to undertake to arrive here, was completely forgotten . . ."

The first signs of decline appeared under the Prussian management of Hardenberg in April 1790. After the death of the Margrave, who had sold his land to Prussia, the fate of the factory was sealed. Eight months of unpaid salaries were entered as debit. The assets on paper totaled 52,730 florins, and

Fig. 55. Pair of Lovers. Ansbach around 1770. Model by Johann Friedrich Kaendler

the debts totaled 21,159 florins. The factory was auctioned off when Ansbach was made part of Bavaria under Napoleon. At the auction the factory was acquired by its second director, C. H. Loewe, who managed it successfully up to 1821, the year of his death. The factory was kept in operation until 1860 but had lost all artistic importance.

KELSTERBACH

The Hesse-Darmstadt factory in Kelsterbach was founded in 1761 on the premises of a bankrupt faience factory. It was in existence for only seven years. Count Ludwig VIII bought it for his son, Georg Wilhelm, and the arcanist Christian Daniel

Fig. 56. Young Girl. Kelsterbach around 1765. Model by Carl Vogelmann

Busch converted it into a porcelain factory. It was enlarged by the addition of a large farm house with roomy cellars for storage space where the paste could be prepared. The former faience factory was spacious enough for the turners, formers, repairers, and painters. Busch became director in 1761 and stayed in Kelsterbach until 1764. He was an arcanist and painter and had acquired his experience in Meissen (around 1745), Vienna, Nymphenburg, Kuenersburg, Bayreuth, Augsburg (1751), Strassburg, and Sèvres (1754–1761). He returned to Meissen in 1765 to replace Hoeroldt and died there in 1790. After his departure *Kabinettkassierer* (Cabinet Treasurer) Pfaff was appointed director.

Carl Vogelmann, perhaps a pupil of Ferdinand Tietz, was the modeler. His groups and figures, seventy altogether, are bizarre creations, and they imparted their imprint on Kelsterbach's style. Their lively dancing poses are quite striking. In the beginning Vogelmann modeled the entire individual figure in unwieldy porcelain paste, and these models show no seams. One of these unique creations representing a very rare but typical Vogelmann figure is illustrated here (Fig. 56). His later figures are cast and repaired in the usual manner. Since his models were few, the individual parts were used for different figures. The body was kept, but different hands and heads were attached, and the legs were given different poses. The figure of the singer has never been mentioned in the literature on Kelsterbach.

Vogelmann's models were repaired by Jakob and Cornelius Carlstadt. We know the names of two other modelers: Eckardt and Freybott. When Vogelmann left in 1767, he was replaced by Peter Anton Seefried, who studied under Bustelli in Nymphenburg. After a short stay in Ludwigsburg he came to Kelsterbach on June 1, 1767. His models are pleasing but their elongated limbs and prominent hips give away his training as a repairer. He had never before done his own modeling and had only assembled the formed parts. Seefried added fifty-five models to Kelsterbach's collection. He returned to Nymphenburg when the Count died in 1769 and when the fate of the factory seemed doubtful. The figures were painted by the well-known Georg Ignaz Hess, son of Georg Friedrich Hess of Fulda (1761–1764). Franz Joseph Weber decorated the few pieces of tableware.

In addition to Hess and Weber, four more names are known: Eger, Ott, Rahner, and Wohlfahrt. None of these stayed longer than a few weeks. Rahner is Georg Conrad Rahner, the skilled painter of flowers and fruit in Frankenthal.

During the short period from January 1766 to the end of 1768, the Count contributed the significant sum of 11,557 florins, and his successor, Ludwig IX, paid debts totaling 658 florins. There is no record of the factory's income.

The production of porcelain came to an end with the death of Count Ludwig VIII. He suffered a stroke while attending the opera in Darmstadt in the company of his beautiful daughter-in-law. The factory was converted later into a faience workshop for the manufacture of inexpensive tableware.

FULDA

The history of the Fulda porcelain factory belonging to Prince Bishop Heinrich von Bibra has never been recorded until now. I have taken my information from a monograph of *Regierungsbaurat* (Commissioner of City Planning) Ernst Kramer in Fulda.

As early as 1741, Prince Abbot Amandus von Buseck gave orders to build a faience factory. Among the specialists he consulted there was Adam Friedrich von Loewenfinck, the fugitive from Meissen whom we know already from Hoechst and Ansbach. Fulda produced true porcelain after 1764 when the arcanist Niklaus Paul arrived in the city, probably through the intervention of Court Councilor Welle's wife. He was paid an initial sum of money for his services from September 15 to October 10, 1764. Paul, who originally had been a master baker, had learned the arcanum when he was employed at the porcelain factory in Hoechst. He knew about the correct mixture of raw materials from Passau and also knew how to design the Vienna kiln. However, not more than one year later, Count von Kassel wooed Paul away with promising proposals. Kaolin had been discovered near the village of Abstroda on the Rhône. Two hundred years later one can still see the remainders of the former deposits. This kaolin was more beautiful than the famous clay from Passau, which had been used by most other factories.

After Paul's departure the new factory was left without an arcanist, but Paul had taught the Prince Bishop's aide, Mayor Schick, how to prepare the paste and how to construct the kiln. Schick in turn taught Abraham Ripp. The factory burned down in 1770 but a loan from the Prince Bishop made it possible to rebuild it. Ripp managed the factory after Schick's death.

Fulda was not a large factory: We know of about one hundred figures and groups produced there. The factory staff consisted of one master modeler, two to three turners for the tableware, two to

Fig. 57. Boy with Two Dogs, near Dog House. Fulda around 1775. Model by G. W. Bartholome

three painters, one underglaze blue painter for the inexpensive tableware and for the marking of dishes, one man for the throwing of the saggers, a glazer, and one man each for the chopping of the fuel wood and for the preparation of the paste. Each factory employed apprentices to secure a new generation of craftsmen, and once they were trained they provided cheap labor. Altogether, there may have been a dozen craftsmen at Fulda who created the rare and very valuable Fulda figures.

Several experts aside from Niklaus Paul worked at Fulda: turners Knittel and Friedrich Ripp, the son of the arcanist and manager; polychrome painters and finishers Peter Angele and Andreas Handschuh, formerly from Frankenthal and son-in-law of the manager; blue painter Birkensee; kiln masters Reichert and Peter Messing; thrower of saggers Hack. The last apprentice was Phillip Hess, born in 1771, son of the porcelain painter Ignaz Hess. He had to be content with one florin pocket money and some clothing. When the factory was closed in 1789, he was appointed cabinet maker. However, after having been boxed in the ear one hundred times within six months—as the records tell us—he left for Ludwigsburg.

Let us go back to the modelers: Johann Georg Schuhmann, Valentin Schaum, Wenzel Neu, and Georg Wilhelm Bartholome. These artists created one hundred models. It is not easy to distinguish the origin of the individual pieces. We know that Schuhmann modeled cane handles and cane buttons, also milk pitchers, kettles, and tea cups. Valentin Schaum had been a wood sculptor previously, and it was he who made the magnificent *Rocailles* in the mirror cabinet of Fulda Castle. The sculptor Schaum worked together with the repairer Johann Andreas Guenther. Guenther's father had been a former in various porcelain factories and was a skilled craftsman. According to the records of the Hoechst factory he was *vasorum hujatis fabricae tornator* (turner of tableware on the potter's wheel). Johann Andreas Guenther moved from Fulda to Kelsterbach in 1766 and later to Fuerstenberg. He is said to have wandered all over Europe.

Schaum modeled the very first figure in Fulda: a messenger boy. The same figure from Frankenthal served as his model. There are more early Fulda figures that had "relatives" in Frankenthal. This is because Prince Bishop von Walderdorff had ordered fifty Frankenthal figures to decorate his splendid rooms in the Fulda Castle. These were later copied in the porcelain factory. Such thefts from other factories were not considered criminal at the time. Wenzel Neu from Bohemia, who had modeled in the

Fig. 58. Peasant Girl and Vintager. Fulda around 1775. Model by G. W. Bartholome

faience factory previously, returned from Closter-Veilsdorf after the porcelain factory opened. His most outstanding work is a Madonna. Bartholome, who had been trained as a repairer, became a modeler of distinction. Although his figures give him away as a former repairer, he was able to make up for this with his creative imagination. One of his models represents a young boy feeding two dogs (Fig. 57). It is a typical Fulda model and the delicate painting adds to its beauty and distinction. Other figures and groups modeled at Fulda include a Peasant Woman and Vintager (Fig. 58) by Bartholome, the pastoral scene *"Le Painier Mystérieux,"* an Apple Harvest, an Amorous Pair with Harlequin.

Fig. 59. Plate and cup decorated with "Classical Portrait." Fulda around 1780. Painted by Peter Angele

There is also a series of musicians grouped together by the modeler to form an orchestra.

The tableware is decorated in the same delicate manner as the figures. Here the flower painter Handschuh created small works of art with a succession of battle scenes, landscapes, animals, birds, and fruit. After the middle of the century, cups with initials in the form of flower garlands and relief "biscuit" medallions were very much in fashion. Very often classical portraits by Peter Angele were painted on plates and cups (Fig. 59).

It was always a tragedy when a factory had to close its doors for the last time. The poor workers usually dispersed in all directions, and they often were without employment for years or had to find work in other occupations which could not do justice to their talents. In Fulda the benevolent Prince Bishop Adalbert provided employment for all his subjects. The painter Angele went to Berlin, Hess to Ludwigsburg, and the Prince Bishop secured positions as butlers, janitors, or artisans for all those who could not find any means of livelihood.

KASSEL

A porcelain factory was founded in Kassel as a result of the ambitions of Count Frederick II. On May 6, 1766, he entrusted its direction to *Kammerpresidenten* (President of the Chamber) Waitz of Eschen and *Domaenenrat* (Councilor of the Domain) Schoenstaedt. It was their responsibility to hire an arcanist who had demonstrated proof of his knowledge. The prison's overseer, Johann Heinrich Schultze, was hired to keep accounts, since he had filled this position in the old faience factory previously. Niklaus Paul of Fulda became the arcanist.

The following idyllic little story will illustrate how one went about recruiting experts from other factories. At the end of February 1766, Inspector Schmidt of Schwarzenfels traveled to Fulda to make secret inquiries concerning the progress accomplished there under Paul. Schmidt wrote on March 8 that he had been in Fulda and that he had succeeded in securing reliable information about the factory from a number of inhabitants within the city and its surroundings. Paul had fired porcelain four times up to now. The porcelain was said to be lovely and equal to Meissen's. He himself had not seen any porcelain, because it was all requisitioned by the court. One could enter the factory only by permission from Director Welle and Mayor Schick; no one else had the key. Through the help of a friend whom he had convinced with a small gift of a few guilders, he had been able to arrange a meeting with the arcanist Paul, who was surprised to see him there. He, Paul, had written many letters to Kassel but they had all been intercepted. Paul had traveled to another part of the country and from there had submitted his demands to the Count by letter. When Schmidt mentioned his desire to see the factory, Paul appeared shocked. Nobody was permitted to enter the premises where the kilns were standing. They were guarded day and night. Paul then asked for fifty florins to pay off his debts in Fulda, as he had not received any salary for three months.

In Kassel Paul demanded and was given, *ad dies vitae* (for life), 450 florins a year, free lodging, eight cords of wood, and fifty pounds of candles. On April 18, 1766, he arrived in Kassel, accompanied by the kiln master and paste mixer Peter Messing. The first firing took place on July 12, 1766, and the kiln was set with knife handles, cane handles, pipe bowls, tobacco boxes—all objects that would present no difficulties in the firing. Messing had much experience and 90 per cent of what was taken out of the kiln after the firing was intact; only nine cups were cracked out of a total of 109.

The Count was pleased with the results of Niklaus Paul's art and the first firing, and now began the search for more experts. Next to the arcanist, the most important man in the factory was the master modeler. Letters of application from craftsmen had been received from Fuerstenberg, Hoechst, Fulda, Ottweiler, Guttenbrunn, Frankenthal, and Sèvres. Director Waitz had personally traveled to Karlshafen with the intention of winning over artists from Fuerstenberg. One hundred eighty people worked there, according to reliable witnesses.

The master modeler and master turner Johann Georg Paland, who had worked in Fuerstenberg for thirteen years, and the former Friedrich Kuenkler arrived unannounced in Kassel on June 21, 1766 and were engaged immediately, although the former was already an "old man." When Fuerstenberg heard the news, there was almost a political rift between the two governments. After lengthy deliberations lasting several days, the two received permission to work in Kassel. When he fled, Paland had left his whole household in Fuerstenberg, but his wife and children had preceded him.

More craftsmen and seven laborers were engaged during the founding year, and in 1788 the number of workmen had risen to one hundred. The best of them were the painters Jacques Dortu, who later founded the second Swiss porcelain factory in Nyon, and Johann Heinrich Eisentraeger, who painted the harlequin scenes on a tea kettle mounted in silver with gold plating (Fig. 60). It was turned by the master turner Paland.

In 1773 a new factory building and a new three-story kiln were put in operation, all at a cost of 980 thalers. To construct the kilns, the following materials were needed: one shipload of building stones, two cartloads of sand, 3,000 bricks of inferior quality, 4,000 bricks of good quality, two cartloads of loam and three fourths of a cartload of chalk. The total cost including wages was thirty-two thalers, which in today's currency would come to roughly 1,300 Swiss francs.

The clay needed for porcelain was bought in Passau and in seven other places. But in spite of excellent results, Kassel shared the fate of the other factories. The management tried to forestall its demise by organizing lotteries. The first lottery drew up the following winning plan: one prize valued at 150 florins, one prize at 100 florins, one prize at 50 florins, one prize at 30 florins. Two thousand lottery tickets were printed with winning numbers from 1 to 600. The first prize was a complete table service with eighteen knives and forks, "heavy silver with gold plating."

The sales promotion then was done much as it is today: in newspapers, through private correspondence, and, of course, through one method much more prevalent then than now—at fairs and through street peddlers. Everyone who traveled through the country and who was engaged in trade needed a passport. Below is an illustration of one of those passports—from the year 1763—belonging to a Kassel factory's faience peddler.

An extensive sales inventory listing hundreds of

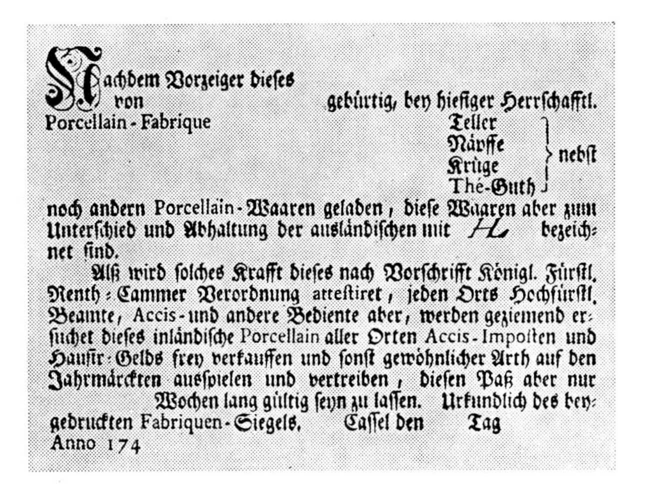
Nachdem Vorzeiger dieses
von   gebürtig, bey hiesiger Herrschafftl.
Porcellain - Fabrique
Teller
Näpffe
Krüge
Thé-Guth } nebst
noch andern Porcellain-Waaren geladen, diese Waaren aber zum Unterschied und Abhaltung der ausländischen mit *H* bezeichnet sind.

Alß wird solches Krafft dieses nach Vorschrifft Königl. Fürstl. Renth-Cammer Verordnung attestiret, jeden Orts Hochfürstl. Beamte, Accis-und andere Bediente aber, werden geziemend ersuchet dieses inländische Porcellain aller Orten Accis-Impolten und Hausir-Gelds frey verkauffen und sonst gewöhnlicher Arth auf den Jahrmärckten ausspielen und vertreiben, diesen Paß aber nur Wochen lang gültig seyn zu lassen. Urkundlich des beygedruckten Fabriquen-Siegels. Cassel den Tag
Anno 174

articles exists from the year 1773. I shall enumerate only the most interesting objects:

Eye cups (to be used for eye baths)
barber basins
casseroles
small rosewater bottles
Crucifixes
handbasins
buttons for waistcoats and jackets
nightlamps
needleboxes
pipe bowls in ten varieties (Jew's face, hussar caps, bear, Moor, tulip, etc.)
rings
cane handles in many shapes ("crawling snake," "with face," etc.)

The figures:

Harlequin; Bear and Bear Hunt; Peasant Woman with Bass Violin; Rabbits and Chamois Goat on Mountain; Europa with Bull; Elephants; figures representing the seasons; Group of Cows; Leopard; salt shaker in the shape of a Moor; Exotic Animals; Zither Player.

Whatever was demanded by the customers was modeled and fired. How very different was the sales inventory of the large factories!

The factory was closed by the monarch on April 27, 1786. This proved impracticable as so much unfinished merchandise was left. And besides, how could one chase away sixty-eight workers and their families? The Count gave definite new orders to keep the factory working for another year, and in the meantime everybody had an opportunity to look for work elsewhere. On January 20, 1787, the factory was offered for sale through the newspapers and was bought by a textile concern. The last workers were given traveling money representing half a week's wages.

WUERZBURG

The porcelain factory of *Konsistorialrath und Geheimen Kanzlisten* (Consistorial Councilor and Privy Chancery Clerk) Johann Caspar Geyger was in existence for exactly five years, from December 1775 to the summer of 1780. With rare exceptions, the tableware and also the figures produced in this factory exhibited defects of varying degrees, proof of the unequal struggle between fire and earth. Nevertheless, these groups are striking in their originality and freshness. Why Geyger, whose time was taken up with so many official functions, opened a porcelain factory remains an unsolved mystery. Wuerzburg was the most unfavorable place for an enterprise of this kind. Surrounding it, within 62 miles (100 kilometers), there were eleven faience and porcelain factories in operation, all selling their wares within the same area. Wuerzburg itself had only 20,000 inhabitants.

The privilege to operate a factory was granted to Geyger by Prince Bishop Adam Friedrich von Seinsheim. Geyger built his factory out of his own funds, before the new gate in the *Loosichen Garten*. In his *Promemoria* Geyger writes that the factory contributed to "the country's honor, His Excellency's advantage and to the benefit of the inhabitants."

As no personnel lists were available, a list of the employees could be found only in the church records, where the trade was usually mentioned next to the name. The following people worked for Geyger: Laurentius Leichard, turner; Ludwig Hof, painter; Georg Briener, turner; Mathias Marabek, kiln master; J. C. Tuennich, miniature-painter; Johann Georg Denkler, master modeler; the "son of a Wuerzburg peasant"; and the apprentice potter Johannes. It seems improbable that Geyger operated his factory with these eight people alone, but no other names could be found.

Geyger offered tableware and figures. The tableware was still very much under the influence of the rococo, even though the Louis XVI style had penetrated to most other factories between 1775 and 1780. It seems that Geyger carried only breakfast sets and coffee and tea services. They were all turned by Leichard who after the closing of the Wuerzburg factory went to Ludwigsburg where he was the *Weissdreher* (turner for white objects). The tableware is decorated with flowers, landscapes, garlands, birds, and the Japanese reed design, and Tuennich seems to have painted most of it. What is missing are the more ambitious paintings, such as scenes after Watteau, battle scenes, genre scenes, and portraits. They made too-high demands on a painter's skill.

The figures are modeled in an original manner

Fig. 60. Tea pot. Decorated with genre scenes. Mounted in gilded silver. Kassel around 1770. Painted by J. Heinrich Eisentraeger

that also marks the molding of the pedestals, the proportions, and the decorations. At times, a figure was deformed to such a degree in the firing that it needed to be supported. Geyger's motifs are taken from everyday life. A maid standing on an earthen socket holding grapes is an allegory of autumn, a youth with sickle and sheaves of corn represents summer, and an old man huddled in rags denotes winter. Pantalone, Capitano, Pierrot, Scaramouche, and Columbine from the *Commedia dell'Arte* all appear. These comedians are of particular importance, and several art historians have attributed them to the great sculptor Ferdinand Tietz. The love scenes are more unassuming: a Hunter and Huntress, a

Fig. 61. Pair of Lovers next to Coffee Table. Wuerzburg 1775–1780

Youth and a Maid pouring tea or coffee (Fig. 61). To prevent them from falling over, this latter pair had to be supported by a column.

The Historical Museum in Bamberg has in its possession two of Tietz's old drawing papers with scattered sketches of comedians. They look exactly like the figures from Geyger's factory. Since these sketches also show the models for the marble statues in Schloss Seehof, it is to be assumed that Tietz did some modeling for Geyger in his free time to earn a few extra guilders. This view has become generally accepted today since Geyger's figures and the ones in the Seehof are exactly the same. Some wooden models by Tietz which have been cast in porcelain also exist, and there may be a connection between the antique gods made of porcelain and the stone statues in the Seehof. Geyger closed his factory in 1780. Because of their primitive charm, the Wuerzburg figures are now valued as precious and rare.

The Factories in Thuringia

The porcelain factories of Thuringia were founded during the second half of the century. Their importance is overshadowed by the large factories which we have described so far. I can only mention the more significant here. The following factories, all within the territory of Thuringia, are called *Waldfabriken* (forest factories):

Gotha (1757, 1763 to now)
Volkstedt (1760 to now)
Closter-Veilsdorf (1760 to now)
Wallendorf (1764 to now)
Gera (1779–1782)
Limbach (1772 to now)
Illmenau (1777–1792)
Grossbreitenbach and Rauenstein

GOTHA

Gotha is the only factory in Thuringia that remained in private hands for decades. Its founder was Baron von Rotberg. The founding year is unknown, but we know that in 1757 Rotberg tried to persuade the arcanist Niklaus Paul to leave Fuerstenberg. A cup that bears the date 1763 and the mark *R* is unmistakable evidence of its existence. Four years later the owner moved his factory beyond the Sundhaeuser Gate and enlarged it considerably. The first workers were Johann Georg Gabel, painter of historical scenes and landscapes; Christian Schulz, painter of flowers and ornaments; Schmidt, who painted every type of decoration; Rueger, landscape painter; and Frey, flower painter. Rotberg leased the factory to Frey for six years (1782–1788). At that point it started to thrive.

In 1770 twelve men were employed, in 1782 twenty, and in 1796 as many as forty. Gotha always made beautiful tableware. It was pure white and without defects. The *Journal des Modes* of 1795 wrote that of all the factories which had sprung up all over Germany, Gotha alone deserved to be mentioned next to Meissen, Berlin, Vienna, and Fuerstenberg.

After Rotberg's death his widow sold the factory to the Crown Prince for 13,000 florins. The Chamberlain Egidius Henneberg was commanded to share the lease and after 1805 became sole leaseholder. The employees were permitted to stay under his management. The factory remained the property of the Henneberg family until 1881, when the brothers Simson bought it. Gotha did not manufacture any figures, and its tableware was similar in decoration to that of the other factories of the eighteenth century.

VOLKSTEDT-RUDOLSTADT

Volkstedt is the only factory that succeeded in producing porcelain without the assistance of an arcanist. Georg Heinrich Macheleid was ingenious enough to solve the problem on his own. Having studied theology at the university, he was a diligent preacher but also attended lectures on physics and chemistry on the side. More and more, the plan to produce true porcelain was taking shape in his mind. He found the solution while experimenting with some sand that his wife was using for her chores in her kitchen. After a long search he found the quarry from which this sand, containing kaolin, had been transported. In 1760 he was ready to ask his sovereign, Count Johann Friedrich von Schwarzburg-Rudolstadt, to grant him a privilege to establish a porcelain factory. This was granted to "Macheleid and Consorts" on October 4, 1760.

The first factory was built in Macheleid's town of Sitzendorf but was moved to Volkstedt-Rudolstadt two years later. The members of the first "consortium" are not known, but it is probable that they belonged to the court. Count Johann Friedrich and his successor, Ludwig Guenther, promoted the enterprise by advancing funds and concessions.

On March 30, 1767, the Volkstedt factory was unexpectedly leased to Christian Nonne. Macheleid was paid off for unknown reasons and received a pension for life as settlement. Nonne was a businessman who knew how to secure orders. He managed the Volkstedt factory for thirty-three years. Its technical and artistic success were due to his initiative. Through all these years kaolin was brought from the deposit where Macheleid had discovered it. The artistic work was done in Volkstedt, but the paste was prepared at its source, in Schaala. The *Praeparatorium*, or paste works, as it was called, was for decades under the supervision of Johann Michael Baering. Although the society had owed a considerable sum to the sovereign in 1769, business was conducted so profitably that it was free of debts in 1775. In 1780 the factory lost its oldest and best artist, the court painter Johann Andreas Greiner. Together with his brother, one of the technical assistants, he secretly bought the porcelain factory in Gera. This led to years of litigation, which finally was settled by a contract consolidating Volkstedt and Gera under common management. However, new difficulties developed repeatedly until in 1799 Volkstedt was bought by the merchants Greiner and Holzapfel who, two years earlier, had bought the porcelain factory in Veilsdorf.

We have only scanty information about the artists at Volkstedt. Around 1770 the factory specialized in small and large wall paintings, portraits of the ladies and gentlemen of the nobility, and landscapes (Fig. 62). One tableau depicts a castle that I presume to be the former Schloss Schwarzburg. Another small plaque bears the inscription, *"fecit Georg Wilhelm Greiner senior Rudolstatt,"* and with it the father of the two Greiners proved that he, too, was an accomplished painter. He was *Hofkommissar* (Court Commissioner) of Rudolstadt. Who were the painters? Besides the court painter Johann Andreas Greiner, Triebner and Reiher are mentioned in the records. Kuenkler from Fuerstenberg was the repairer during the early years. The court painter Cotta seems to have been the foremost artist during the later years.

These are the few reliable details available on the artistic staff at Volkstedt. The factory turned out everything that was manufactured at the other factories: tableware in all shapes and at all prices, some plain and unpainted, some with the inexpensive underglaze blue onion pattern, and some gilded services with fine polychrome decorations for the court. Volkstedt produced large fireplace vases, mounted on brackets depicting standing soldiers and figures. Compared to Meissen, the figures were of poor quality, and the modeler is not known. Next to the pictures, white biscuit busts were a specialty. The factory is still in operation today under the name *Aelteste Volkstedter Porzellanfabrik*.

CLOSTER-VEILSDORF

Porcelain must have been manufactured in Veilsdorf for thirty-seven years before the sale to the brothers Greiner took place on February 12, 1797. An old ledger sheet showing entries of wages is dated August 11, 1760.

The founder was Prince Friedrich Wilhelm Eugen von Hiltburghausen, the brother of the reigning Duke Ernst Friedrich Carl von Sachsen Hiltburghausen. Johann Hermann Meyer was the arcanist. The kaolin was bought in Passau and mixed with local clay. Veilsdorf was foremost among the factories in Thuringia for its artistic quality. The direction was in the hands of the Prince's trusted adviser, Johann Ernst Bayer, and the manager was Friedrich Doell. No other patron was as actively involved in his factory and its workers as Prince Eugen. He worked on the development of colors and glazes himself, bought copper engravings for the modelers, and drafted designs. But above all, he stimulated interest in his merchandise among the nobility and at court.

Gradually, after the first porcelain had been fired in 1763, the factory expanded, and six years later fifty persons were employed. From 1777 onward, Prince Eugen entertained a lively correspondence with his assistant, Bayer, and the entire history of this interesting factory can be learned from it. The list of employees contains some well-known names, such as Niklaus Paul and his son. Wherever father Paul appeared, the production of true porcelain followed. Ripp, della Torre, and the modeler Wenzel Neu also worked here. The first ware was turned by Johann Nuernberger who later appeared in Wallendorf. "The first Rococo services of the Veilsdorf factory are pleasantly noteworthy for their tasteful forms and their delicate painting" (Graul). The painting on a 10 in. (25 cm) tall coffee pot (Fig. 63)

Fig. 62. Two small plaques. Volkstedt-Rudolstadt around 1770. One of them painted by Georg Wilhelm Greiner, senior

Fig. 63. Coffee pot decorated with medallion and light brown genre scene. Volkstedt around 1765–1770. Probably painted by Friedrich Doell after an engraving by Weyroter

is particularly lovely. For its decoration Prince Eugen chose an engraving from the series *Deuxième Suite des Ruines et Paysages, dessinés après nature et gravés par Weyroter* (illustration, opposite page).

The small painting, with its light colors, is typical for Veilsdorf. The engraving is dated 1765, and the painting was done during the factory's early years. There were ten different painters working in Veilsdorf around 1765. The son of manager Friedrich Doell was the most accomplished. We should also mention the brothers Dressel, who were excellent painters. One of them appears in Limbach in 1778.

Veilsdorf also was famous for its figures among the factories in Thuringia. Unfortunately, only the names of the modelers are known—not their models. The factory sent theatrical figures and allegorical figures representing the planets to a merchant in Mannheim as early as 1767. Each piece cost eight florins. We can recognize the theatrical figures from the designs used by the Veilsdorf modelers: Scaramouche with his lute, Dottore, Gabriel, Capitano, Columbine and Harlequin, Pantalone, Mezzetin and Pierrot—the entire company of the old *Commedia dell'Arte,* taken from a series of engravings by Balthasar Probst after Johann Jakob Schuebler's *Amor vehementer.*

The figures of a Persian and a Sultan (Fig. 64) illustrated here come from Veilsdorf, too. The first, Cyrus, was modeled by Franz Kotta in 1778. The second, the Sultan, was modeled by F. W. E. Doell in 1769 from an engraving by Ferriol. Doell later became court sculptor in Gotha.

The rich variety of objects included everything that was regarded as indispensable to an elegant household of the eighteenth century: figures used for table decorations and show cases, shepherds and shepherdesses, vintagers, peasants, a Beggar Woman with Basket and Cane, allegories representing the seasons, a Venus, comedians, figures in various costumes, gods and goddesses.

Fig. 64. Persian King and "Grandsultan in the Serail." Closter-Veilsdorf 1767. After an engraving by Ferriol, 1714

The Veilsdorf factory was sold in 1797 for 15,000 florins. It went to the sons of Gotthelf Greiner in Limbach and to Friedrich Christian Greiner in Rauenstein. This brought an end to the artistic period, as the Greiners manufactured only utilitarian industrial merchandise.

WALLENDORF

The first to experiment with the manufacture of true porcelain was the leaseholder of the Count's smelting works in Katzhuette, Johann Wolfgang Hammann. In collaboration with the court potter Johann Georg Duemmler and the glass blowers Gotthelf Greiner and Gottfried Greiner, Hammann discovered the secret formula. The first firing, in 1762, was successful. Prince von Schwarzburg, in whose territory Katzhuette was situated, forbade any further experiments, and consequently the four men were forced to leave the country. Hammann was able to settle in Koburg-Saalfeld. He bought the Wallendorf estate for 90,000 florins and it became the seat of the factory of the same name. Prince Franz Josias granted them a privilege on March 30, 1764.

The company was founded by Hammann, his son, his brother, and the two arcanists mentioned above, Johann Gottfried and Gotthelf Greiner. Seven years later Gotthelf Greiner withdrew and founded the Limbach factory.

In the years 1764 and 1765 Hammann employed thirty-seven people and this number remained constant to the end of the factory. In 1782 its ownership was transferred to the son, Ferdinand Friedrich Hammann. The factory remained in the family Hammann until it was sold to Hutschenreuter in 1829.

The workers came from the surroundings and also from other factories in Thuringia. Among the painters were Gottlieb Heintze and Johann August Horn. We also find the name of Carl Gottlieb Grahl, the only one about whom some information could be found and whose progress to Wallendorf could be traced. At the end of 1767 he was director in Ottweiler and later a painter in Kassel. He disappeared again on October 2, 1770 without giving notice and went directly to Meissen, where he was engaged to teach the young painters. Of Heintze and Horn we only know the names. Both names, however, with different first names, are also recorded in Meissen.

The next personnel roster is dated 1794. Among the turners there appears a Johann Georg Horn, probably the son of the painter Johann August. Of particular interest is the former Gabriel Klein. On February 8, 1785, in the church of Kilchberg near Zurich, a boy was christened Hansjakob, son of "the factory worker Gabriel Klein from Lingenwil [Luneville] in Lothringen and his wife Margaretha Ischoli." In 1785 Klein worked as turner, former, repairer, and modeler in the Zurich porcelain factory. In Luneville he was employed in the factory of the widow Chambrette. The famous modeler Paul Louis Cyffle sold the factory in 1788 and many artists moved away. Klein went to Zurich and remained there until 1790, during which year the Zurich factory went bankrupt. It is not clear why he came to Wallendorf, but he worked there from 1794 to 1800. He modeled figures, as he had done in Zurich, earning 155 thalers in 1794, 188 thalers in 1796, 220 thalers in 1797, and as much as 251 thalers in 1798. Klein was the best-paid modeler, and his co-worker Johann Georg Sontag received only a little more than half that salary. In 1805 he was in Gieshuebel, where he died in 1818. Like Klein, many porcelain workers wandered from one country to another to find a new home wherever a position became vacant.

Wallendorf manufactured more comedians but the name of the artist is unknown. One Columbine figure is dated 1783. One of the most charming Wallendorf groups is a Pair with Bird's Nest (Fig. 65) from the period around 1770. It is modeled after an engraving by Amiconi (illustration, left).

Wallendorf, as all the other *Waldfabriken,* manu-

Fig. 65. Youth and Maid with Bird's Nest. Wallendorf around 1770, after an engraving by J. Amiconi

factured tableware for all classes, and especially for the less affluent. In 1791 there were sixty-nine firings in the old kiln and seventy-seven in the new kiln, a total of 146. These figures are almost incredible. If in addition we consider the quantities produced at each firing, we come to the conclusion that there must have been a total production of about 50,000 pieces a year. In 1797 the two kilns held, among other things, sixty dozen cups and saucers, twenty-two coffee pots, thirty milk pitchers, ten tea pots, sixteen sugar bowls, seventeen wash basins, five spittoons, twenty-three bird whistles (for dogs), and 1,400 *Tuerkenkoppchen,* which were shipped to Turkey. As far as export was concerned, Wallendorf was one of the leading factories of the eighteenth century. The factory is still in existence today.

LIMBACH

Gotthelf Greiner, one of the co-founders of the Wallendorf porcelain factory, built his own factory in Limbach in 1772. He had experimented with porcelain for a number of years before his stay in Wallendorf and had succeeded in producing a few poorly-glazed pipe bowls. He lacked the funds for a larger enterprise. After acquiring experience and some capital in Wallendorf, he felt encouraged to build a factory of his own in Limbach. On November 10, 1772, the first firing took place in his new kiln. His biography states: "We carried the porcelain ware solemnly and placed it in the kiln. The fire was burning well. My fears vanished and long awaited exultation took its place. I watched the kiln myself to the completion of the firing, and thank God the results were excellent."

Well-decorated pieces are rare. One of the oldest objects may be a barber bowl (Fig. 66) dated 1778 which on the reverse bears the mark of the factory, "LN," and the signature of the painter Dressel, all in iron-red. On the *cartouche* held by two putti with flying ribbons, the monogram "GM" appears. On the border, in an oval formed by leaves, is a hammer and vise. The design is original, but the quality of the painting is not outstanding. The piece is interesting because of the date and the signature.

Between 1774 and 1800, Limbach employed seventy-one workers, among them two kiln masters, sixteen turners, one former, four repairers, twenty-seven painters, and ten *Fabrikanten* (laborers). In 1775 others arrived from different factories. Johann Caspar Frede came from Fuerstenberg, where he had been an apprentice former from 1767 to 1772 and later a former. Then came Johann Carl Ens, the painter from Ansbach who was the ancestor of the porcelain-manufacturing Ens families in Thuringia. Michael Kaup, the gilder, is mentioned as having come from Ludswigsburg. The painter of the barber bowl, Heinrich Elias Dressel, came to Limbach in 1778. This barber bowl was quite obviously his first porcelain piece, one which he had to paint to prove his skill shortly after his arrival in Limbach.

Limbach's figures are rare compared to the tableware. While the ornamentation on the tableware was not of outstanding quality up to the end of the eighteenth century, the figures are probably among the best produced by any of the factories in Thuringia. Even so, a certain provincial trait can be detected in the figures. Their origin cannot be denied: obviously, the society of citizens and peasants served as models for the artists. Also produced were allegories of the seasons, putti with their distinguishing marks—in short, everything we have encountered in the other factories as well. The figures can be attributed to three different modelers: Caspar Jensel for the early period; Heumann, who started working in Limbach in 1778; and finally Kinzel, who arrived in 1786.

Five years before his death, Greiner entrusted the factory to his five sons. Each had received excellent training from him. The factory was in operation up to the end of the nineteenth century.

Fig. 66. Barber bowl. Limbach 1778. Painted by Dressel

SWITZERLAND

Zurich

Switzerland had two porcelain factories during the eighteenth century, the first founded in 1763 at Zurich, and the second in 1781 at Nyon on Lake Geneva. Among the porcelain factories of the eighteenth century, the Zurich factory occupies a special place because it manufactured simultaneously porcelain, *pâte-tendre,* biscuit, faience, *terre de pipe,* and stoneware. Records of requests to the city council of Zurich tell us why the honorable citizens of that city wanted to have their own factory. "Rather in the hope and with the best intention to be of service to their country, than for profit-seeking speculations," they were moved to "dare this enterprise and build a factory. To this time this had only been possible in places where either the sovereign took its execution upon himself or favored the establishment with special privileges and grants. It had further been considered to create a means of livelihood and support for many citizens who, because of various infirmities, were not fit for any other work." The intentions of the citizens of Zurich were therefore most noble and merited the council's consent.

Among the founders were Salomon Gessner, Martin Usteri, Heinrich Lavater, Conrad Voegeli, Felix Corrodi, and Hans Conrad Heidegger. All were members of the Naturalist Society, which still exists today. Gessner was a member of the city council and the owner of a print shop, *Zum Schwanen.* Martin Usteri lived in Talhof and was a merchant, while Heinrich Lavater became mayor in 1768. Corrodi was a painter and county clerk and Voegeli was librarian.

On August 10, 1763, this *Handelssocietaet* (commerce society) bought the country home of Regula Holzhalb in Schooren at the shore of the lake in Bendikon. (This house is still standing, and in accordance with its tradition it is being carefully preserved by its owners.) The price of the house was 1,450 florins. The village brook of Thalwil operated the grinding mill. Clay was bought in Passau until 1775 and later in Limoges, although it was not inexpensive to transport clay over these distances.

It is possible that the people in Zurich received the arcanum from Ringler who, as we know, wandered all over Europe, and true porcelain was produced wherever he made his appearance. After 1759 he had settled in a secure position in Ludwigsburg, and nothing prevented him from selling the arcanum once again.

The staff consisted of able men. Adam Spengler from Schaffhausen, the director, had been director and faience painter in Franz Rudolf Frisching's faience factory in Bern. There was the painter Johannes Daffinger from Vienna, the modeler Joseph Nees from Memmingen; the floral painter Johann Bonlander, also from Memmingen; the landscape painter Heinrich Thomann from Zollikon; the potter Franz Ludwig Frei from Brugg; the painter Johann Friedrich Bleuler of Zollikon; Johann Bleuler, also from Zollikon, who painted flowers, fruit, and insects; the painter Diethelm Weber from Zurich, later in Ludwigsburg; Heinrich Fuessli of Horgen, painter; the potter Matthias Neeracher of Staefa, who after 1792 became the second owner of the Zurich porcelain factory. Johann Wilhelm Spengler, son of the director, was the modeler. When Spengler became father of an illegitimate child, he had

Fig. 67. Coffee pot. Zurich around 1770. Painted after an engraving by Nilson

to leave Kilchberg. He then spent some time in England, but disappeared without leaving any trace. Also employed were Gabriel Klein of Luneville, modeler; Johannes Meier, repairer, later in Ludwigsburg; Johann Valentin Sonnenschein, modeler from Ludwigsburg; and Caspar Furrer, Hans Heinrich Weerlin, Hans Caspar Eschmann-Hochstrasser, Hans Jakob Scheller, and Caspar Maurer, whose specialties are not known. It is obvious that every department was well covered.

A plate with landscape (Fig. 68) may serve as an example of the Zurich production. It has a width of 12 inches (31.5 cm) and was painted by Heinrich Thomann after an engraving by Salomon Gessner. The quality of the painting done in Zurich is among the best produced in all the porcelain factories of the eighteenth century. This plate, showing a ruin at the rocky shores of a river and grazing cattle, conveys the idyllic content of the Swiss poetry of the time.

Even so, the factory had to promote its wares.

Fig. 68. Platter. Zurich around 1770–1780. Painted by Heinrich Thomann after an engraving by Salomon Gessner

Martin Usteri was entrusted with the commercial aspect of the enterprise, but he had to contend with much criticism. "His pride, his nonsensical *point d'honneur* to carry every project to its conclusion regardless of cost, these are the dominating traits of Usteri and the cause of our misfortunes," Heinrich Gessner once wrote to Caspar Zellweger.

The opening of the factory on April 19, 1764 was announced by Spengler in the *Zuercher Donnstagblatt.* In the beginning, Usteri sold faiences only in the Muensterhof. In 1768, thirty-two florins were paid for the vault under the Meise, the same place where today the Landesmuseum displays its Zurich porcelain. It seems that Usteri was replaced in 1768 by the shopkeeper and button manufacturer Johann Conrad Waser. He was member No. 169 of the *Saffranzunft* (Saffron Guild) and *Commissaer allhiesiger Porcellainfabrique* (Commissioner of all Porcelain Factories in the Region). During that summer he sold from his shop under the Meise, and in the winter from the Badergasse (today Zinngasse). In addition, Adam Spengler's son-in-law, Salomon Keller, traded with porcelain merchandise from the porcelain factory at Niederdorf in the Graebliggasse. The exquisitely painted tall coffee pot (Fig. 67) shown here was probably sold by Conrad Waser. It was painted after the engraving by J. E. Nilson, *Qua cernunter temporis sunt . . . ,* which was published in Augsburg in 1760 (Schuster, No. 112). A pilgrim with cloak taking a young girl's hand attempts to lead her away from the vanities of this world toward solitude. The original engraving has the following caption: "The signpost serves in leading us along the right path toward the desired goal. However, this world full of vanity tricks us into the opposite direction." An inventory dated 1768 lists the merchandise sent to Weerlin, the stockkeeper during that year, and what he sold. And we also find the prices for several objects: a figure, size four, cost ten florins; a smaller one, No. 2, was only 2 florins 30 xr. A Herr Grasset of Lausanne bought twenty-seven figures, No. 2, in 1768 for a total price of 67 florins 30 xr. The smallest figures, No. 1, still cost 1 florin 10 xr.

Here, too, they tried to dispose of merchandise by means of lotteries. Spengler conducted one of these in 1773 with 30,057 pieces. This enormous number

Fig. 69. Table centerpiece with Bacchus on the Barrel. Zurich around 1775. Model probably by Valentin Sonnenschein

shows that production exceeded demand by far. We have no record of the proceeds from this lottery.

The Zurich city council presented the Einsiedel Monastery with a large dinner service. During a litigation between Zurich and Schwyz concerning the fishing and shipping rights on the Upper Zurich Lake, the monastery had been host to the Zurich delegation for weeks. The service cost 1,525 florins and 4 Batzen. Part of this service is still on exhibit in the Meise in Zurich.

In addition to services, Zurich also modeled numerous figures. The table centerpiece illustrated (Fig. 69) is probably Sonnenschein's creation. He came to Zurich from Ludwigsburg in 1775 and he had modeled similar neo-classical groups in that city. In the base there are two grottoes for the panthers; four faun musicians are seated at the four corners, while Bacchus on a wine barrel swings a wine-filled beaker. This centerpiece was the largest model manufactured in Zurich and served as evidence that every technical challenge could be mastered in Schooren. The themes represented by the figures were wide ranging. Zurich, too, manufactured comedians, traveling folk, beggars, street singers and musicians, allegorical figures representing the seasons, shepherds and shepherdesses, street criers—everything that presented itself to the modeler in everyday life.

Two servant figures are particularly charming models (Fig. 71). The man is holding a bottle of wine, while the girl is carrying a tray set for breakfast with a so-called solitaire, consisting of cup and saucer, sugar bowl and creamer, and a small coffee pot. Both figures are painted with much taste and care. This holds true for all the Zurich porcelain figures. They were porcelain masterpieces, like the Zurich tableware.

After director Spengler's death the *Handelssocietaet* decided to liquidate the factory. The state of its finances was precarious, and none of the partners were willing to invest any money of their own in the business.

I shall illustrate this sad event by quoting from a letter written by Salomon Gessner's widow to Johann Caspar Zellweger-Gessner: "You must assume that I am near death or in deepest despair. Thank God I have been spared both, but not without a miracle. For fourteen misery-filled days I faced the danger of losing my hard-earned property, the honor of my great late husband, the reputation of my two innocent sons, and the loss of my homeland. These were indeed burdens weighing heavily on my body and soul. For three weeks I foresaw the ruin of every household in Zurich but I was spared our own. . . . Judith Gessner, née Heidegger."

The liquidation lasted for an entire year. The assets totaled 14,600 florins but the debts had mounted to 237,838 florins. Citizens of Basel and Zurich were among the creditors. All debts were finally paid by the shareholders and in 1792 the factory was bought by Mathias Neeracher, a potter from Staefa. He manufactured faiences only, decorated with flowers and inscriptions in the style of the nineteenth century.

Nyon

This porcelain factory in the western part of Switzerland was the last to be founded during the eighteenth century. When Jacques Dortu and Ferdinand Mueller opened the factory on March 12, 1781, the brilliance of the splendor of porcelain was already fading. Only one year later Dortu sold his share for 1,000 gold louis to Mueller and departed for Berlin.

When it became known in April 1787 that Mueller harbored plans to transfer the factory to Geneva, he was banished from Nyon and the patrons recalled the expert Dortu from Berlin. Dortu then managed the factory up to its liquidation in 1813. We know of only a few artists who worked there during the eighteenth century: Etienne Gide, painter; Johann Kaspar Maurer from Adliswil near Zurich; Josef Perneaux from Ludwigsburg, painter of garlands; Wilhelm Rath from Fuerstenberg; and Zinkernagel, who acted as director during Dortu's absence.

A few remarks on the best of Nyon's artists: Ferdinand Charles Mueller came to Nyon together with Dortu. From various records we know that he had been in Frankenthal, Tournai, Ponteux, Lille, Nymphenburg, Capo di Monte, and Mannheim. He was obviously one of those roving *Porcelliner,* and he

Fig. 70. Large vase, mounted in bronze. Nyon around 1790. Probably painted by Etienne Gide after a picture of the city of Lausanne

was accompanied by four different wives. It is not known whether he was actually married to all of them! Etienne Gide is the most famous of the Nyon painters. He was born in Geneva in 1761 and died in 1804. He is even better known for his enamel painting. Dortu hired him in 1789. Perneaux was born in Ludwigsburg in 1772, the son of the master turner. He went to Nyon in 1790 and moved on to Sèvres in 1804. Rath was "junior" painter in Fuerstenberg in 1757 and he earned 120 thalers in 1767. He worked in Nyon as an excellent landscape painter from 1786 to 1801.

Nyon manufactured great quantities of porcelain, but the rococo era was past. The art of porcelain, so beloved and treasured during the eighteenth century, was dealt a death blow when Winkelmann wrote: "Most porcelain is in the shape of ridiculous dolls. From it originated the childish taste which has become so widespread. In its place we should strive to emulate the eternal works of classical art." This view pointed to the direction in which style would develop after 1780. Today we appreciate the porcelain creations of the eighteenth century for their novel and artistic value.

Fig. 71. Man servant and maid servant. Zurich 1770–1775

In 1799 Nyon produced merchandise worth 75,000 livres, and the cost of production was 51,000 livres. Consequently, there was a profit of 24,000 livres if everything was sold. In 1799 the factory sold porcelain for 30,000 livres in Switzerland and for 5,000 livres abroad, and therefore could record no profit. We find names of clients from Bern, Geneva, Amsterdam, Hamburg, London, Marseilles, Turin, and St. Petersburg. The design of the tableware was modern and carefully executed. A good example is a large vase (Fig. 70) decorated with a view of Lausanne. It has two bronze handles and a modern socket.

Nyon's style has been copied again and again. A cup in the Victoria and Albert Museum in London is the modest remainder of a small collection of Nyon tableware; everything else is modern. No doubt, all ceramics museums exhibit Nyon cups which have been painted only recently. During the nineteenth century, factories in Thuringia sold porcelain marked with a fish (the mark of Nyon). It was easy to copy the scattered flowers and garlands, and the factory was often plagued by counterfeiters. The decorations of Nyon are neo-classical: ribbons, laurel wreaths, medallions and Watteau scenes, allegorical scenes, modest blue cornflowers, small bouquets, monograms, trophies, silhouettes, small birds, chinoiseries, musical instruments; in short, all the subjects supplied by the engravers of the Louis XVI period. In Nyon, too, engravings were copied.

However, Nyon fared no better than most other factories of the eighteenth century. In 1813 it had to extinguish the fire in its kiln for good, although the debts of 180,503 livres were almost covered by its assets, including the factory buildings and stock. There was tableware valued at 96,400 livres, but the cash boxes were empty. Thus the second Swiss porcelain factory shared the fate of Zurich and many other factories.

FRANCE

Until 1772, all French factories manufactured only soft-paste porcelain, so-called *pâte-tendre*. It is made of quartz, saltpeter, soda, alum, salt, and gypsum or alabaster. Kaolin was missing. *Pâte-tendre* is a complicated mixture which has to be fired for fifty hours, then pulverized and worked into a plastic paste by the addition of clay and soap. The glaze contains lead, and in the firing the colors blend with it and acquire a magnificent luminosity. The individual factories, in chronological order according to their founding years, were:

Rouen, 1673	Mennecy, 1738
St. Cloud, 1677	Vincennes-Sèvres, 1738
Lille, 1711	Sceaux, 1749
Chantilly, 1725	Arras, 1770

The discovery in 1765 of the kaolin deposit in St. Yrieix near Limoges was an important event.

Rouen

On October 1, 1673, Louis Poterat, son of the faience worker Edmé Poterat in Rouen, received a privilege *"de faire de la véritable porcelaine de Chine"* (to manufacture the true porcelain of China). The very rare jars of Rouen are of heavy paste, not translucent, and painted in cobalt blue, in the style of the faiences of the day. Louis Poterat died in 1696, and with him the first French soft-paste porcelain factory came to an end. Poterat justly holds the title *"premier porcelainier de France"* (first porcelain maker of France).

St. Cloud

Poterat modeled and fired his few porcelain vessels by himself. St. Cloud was the first French factory which, as an industrial enterprise, produced series of objects. Aside from the inventor Pierre Chicaneau, who was also a faience worker, numerous employees worked in the factory. Their names are known exclusively from church records. They are turners, kiln masters, and painters. St. Cloud may owe the secret of its manufacture to a workman from Rouen. After Chicaneau's death, his widow remarried in 1678, and her second husband was another faience worker, Henri Charles Trou, who was a protégé of the Duke of Orleans. He received a privilege from the King's brother in 1702. When the factory was completely destroyed by fire in 1737, Trou rebuilt it and became its sole owner. After his death, his son Henri François succeeded him, and two years later Choudard des Forges, who then liquidated the whole enterprise in 1766.

What did St. Cloud produce? The famous English physician and mineralogist Martin Lister visited the factory in 1698 while traveling through France and wrote: "I have seen the pottery of St. Cloud, and I am very pleased with it, because I have not found any difference between the articles produced in that establishment and the most beautiful porcelain of China that I have seen . . ." An honorable testimony indeed! In St. Cloud there were goblets, mustard pots, egg cups, tea and coffee sets, small vases and potpourris, and also figures and groups which are extremely rare today. Most St. Cloud objects are

Fig. 72. Bottle vase, *pâte tendre*. Saint Cloud around 1700

painted in blue, but there exist a few polychrome pieces of porcelain.

The bottle vase illustrated here (Fig. 72) bears this blue decoration, which was typical for most of the soft-paste porcelain of Rouen and St. Cloud. The ornaments are in the Louis XV style practiced by the French engravers of the period, especially by Berain. The vase is dated "around 1700"—before the invention of true kaolin porcelain by Boettger.

Lille

The tableware of Lille, like St. Cloud's, is made of soft-paste porcelain. It is difficult to distinguish it from the porcelain produced in St. Cloud, since shapes and decorations were identical in both factories. In 1708 there were in Lille the faience works belonging to Barthélémy Dorez and his nephew Pierre Péllissier. Three years later, the city council granted them a privilege for the manufacture of porcelain. They built their factory on the grounds of an old sugar refinery. Péllissier retired in 1716 and Dorez's two sons joined their father. They gave up the manufacture of porcelain in 1730, but the faience factory was in existence until 1790.

Chantilly

In 1725 Louis Henri de Bourbon founded one of the largest French faience factories at Chantilly in the Department Oise. Large buildings were erected outside the city. Chantilly also made only soft-paste porcelain. Ciquaire Cirou, the director, had acquired his knowledge in St. Cloud. He worked together with the brothers Dubois and with Gravant senior and his son, who later became director, and the modeler Louis Fournier. Owners and directors changed eight times up to 1800.

Chantilly employed a large staff:

Louis Goujou, sculptor from Rouen, after 1737 in Chantilly;

Charles Butteux, painter, after 1752; went to Sèvres four years later;

Jean-Jacques Anthéaume, painter, came from Sèvres in 1753 and returned there the following year;

Pierre Dubuisson, fan merchant; in Chantilly in 1753, went to Sèvres the same year, where he was called a floral painter; he escaped from Sèvres and was punished by imprisonment in the Bastille for eight months;

Etienne Gobin of Luneville and Strassburg, where

Fig. 73. Covered bowl. Chantilly around 1740. Decorated after a Korean of Meissen model

he had worked as a floral painter. He, too, left for Sèvres after a short time;

Jacques Matthieu, painter since 1765; he left the factory when he became director of Seynie in 1777.

Here, as in the German factories, artists traveled from city to city, frequently only to earn one more louis. The main "customer" of all these artists was Vincennes and later Sèvres. Chantilly produced the type of porcelain ware which was in demand for the ordinary household: table services; cache-pots; bottle coolers with handles shaped like dragons, salamanders, or dogs' heads; basins and pitchers in all shapes and sizes; incense burners. There were no less than twenty-nine differently molded plates, covered cheese dishes, chamber pots, and much more.

The ornamentation was done with great care. Imitations of Japanese and Chinese designs were typical. A contemporary account says: "The porcelain produced imitates that of Japan so perfectly that some pieces cannot be distinguished from the real." A covered bowl (Fig. 73) with a faithful copy of a Korean design is one of these imitations of Japanese porcelain. Because of its tin glaze we know that it is from the early period around 1740. Later objects have a lead glaze. The same decorative pieces are found in Meissen, too, and it is probable that all Meissen designs were well known in Chantilly. Louis Henri de Bourbon was a great collector and well aware of what was preferred by the first European factory of hard-paste porcelain. Along with tableware, Chantilly modeled figures, mainly chinoiseries. At times they were mounted on bronze sockets or combined with a clock.

Mennecy

François Barbin built his porcelain factory in 1738 in the rue de Charonne in Paris. When in 1748 he applied for permission to build a new kiln, he was ordered to move his factory elsewhere because of the privileges granted to Vincennes. The Duke of Villeroy was interested in Barbin's plans and gave him permission to build the factory in Mennecy in one of the outer buildings on the palace grounds. Barbin named his product *"Porcelaine de Villeroy."*

In 1753 he managed his factory together with his son Jean Baptist. Father and son both died, one shortly after the other, in the year 1765. J. Julien and S. Jacques bought the factory; they had had a similar enterprise in Sceaux. Both appear to have been experienced craftsmen. Julien was a painter, Jacques a sculptor. When their *Permission de Domicile* expired in 1773, they moved their factory to Bourg-la-Reine. Julien died one year later, and Jacques' son Léon became a partner.

The porcelain of Mennecy does not differ in composition from the porcelain of the other French factories. The production consisted of figures and tableware. Barbin formed the tableware in an entirely new manner, and only very few pieces were copied from Meissen's. They are carefully painted, often in the style of Sèvres, as the lovely sugar bowl in the Victoria and Albert Museum in London (Fig. 74) shows. The small bouquet of flowers adds a festive look to the cream-colored body. The production of figures was no less significant: Chinese figures, Callot dwarfs, all kinds of small animals, swans, dogs, monkeys, lions, etc. They are charming miniatures. Particularly precious vases, called *brûle parfums,* were decorated with delicate porcelain flowers on long bronze stems.

Bourg-la-Reine continued its production in the same manner during its first years, but very soon it encountered difficulties as well and after a short time only tea sets with superficial decorations were sold.

Vincennes-Sèvres

Emil Tillman called Sèvres *"un des plus beaux fleurons de la grandeur française"* (one of the loveliest flowers of the greatness of France), and with good reason. The factory was called officially *Manufacture Royale des Porcelaines de France.* Its magnificent products created the keenest competition for Meissen. Mme. de Pompadour, Mme. Du Barry, and all of France took an active interest in its flourishing artistic development. In the estate of the *Protectrice des Arts,* as Mme. de Pompadour was called, there was Sèvres porcelain in the value of 150,000 louis, an enormous sum. Mme. Du Barry in her memoirs enumerates the finest pieces of porcelain bought by her or presented to her by the King. After her death, the rarest and most valuable porcelains were declared national works of art, among them two vases with light blue background, two vases formed in Etruscan style, a barometer and a thermometer, each with porcelain ornamentation and precious painting, a table made of Sèvres porcelain, a commode with porcelain inlay, and a painting by Vanloo on a porcelain plaque. I mention these pieces to illustrate how highly porcelain from Vincennes-Sèvres was valued even then.

In 1738 two craftsmen from Chantilly, the turner Robert Dubois and his brother Gilles, a painter, offered their services to the Minister of Finance, Orry de Fulvi. Both had acquired enough experience to manage a porcelain factory independently. Their request was granted. The King gave orders to put part of the Castle of Vincennes at their disposal. They received financial backing in the amount of 10,000 louis. Since they were drunk every day and couldn't deliver anything but the most deficient ware, the old faience worker François Gravant (1741–1765) replaced them. De Fulvi's valet, Charles Adam, was made director. The King granted a privilege for the manufacture of *façon de Saxe* (Saxon type) as it was called.

Fig. 74. Sugar bowl with lid and spoon. Mennecy around 1760

A company of twenty-one shareholders was made responsible for the financing. Charles Adam had 90,000 louis to work with. Gravant was paid 24,000 louis for his arcanum and was promised a pension for his wife.

After de Fulvi's death in 1751, Baptiste Machault succeeded him as Minister of Finance. He was a very special patron of the factory. At the same time, the chemist Hellot was hired along with the art expert Hulst. Mme. de Pompadour also took an active part in judging the beauty and design of the planned models. The King's goldsmith, Duplessis, supervised the production of the white paste and drew the designs. He also was the inventor of biscuit. The sculptor Bachelier was head of the decoration studio. Thus Vincennes began its manufacture with the assistance of the foremost French experts of its time.

A few more artists deserve mention. Capelle supervised the firing of colors in 1748 and was still in Vincennes in 1779. The former Bulidon came from Chantilly, and from St. Cloud the master gilder Massers. For all workers a standing order of seven points was drawn up which circumscribed their rights and above all their duties. Flight was punishable by imprisonment.

The premises in Vincennes soon became too small

Fig. 76. Small tureen with lid and saucer. *"Bleu de Roi."* Sèvres 1774. Painted by Morain, gilded by Le Gai

and the factory was moved to Sèvres in 1753. This meant proximity to the King and Mme. de Pompadour, who resided in the Bellevue Palace.

Hellot was the inventor of Sèvres' magnificent colors: a dark blue in 1749, the light *bleu céleste* in 1752, then a green, a gray, and—most famous in our time—*rose Pompadour*.

These colors are illustrated in figures 75 and 76. The two small plaques are painted in the precious rose color. The tureen has a dark blue background, the *bleu de roi*. The date 1774 appears on the barrel depicted on the plate. Dated pieces are especially important because they give evidence of the artistic style of an entire period. The tureen was painted by Morain, *"peintre des marines et subjets militaires,"* and it was gilded by Le Gai. It is signed "M" and "LG" at the base.

There were painters who specialized in flowers, others in fruit, birds, and landscapes, and during their stay at Vincennes they were not permitted to paint anything but their specialties. Porcelain flowers were a particular specialty, and in 1750 these were sold for 16,000 louis, which represented two thirds of the total income. Forty-five women were occupied with their production. Mme. de Pompadour received Louis XV in her winter garden with 470

Fig. 75. Two small plaques. *Rose Pompadour* background. Sèvres around 1755–1760

porcelain flowers, each one perfumed with its own scent. The so-called *oeil-de-perdrix* (small dotted circles) and the unnatural jewel porcelain (melted gold pallets and pearls) were favorite designs. Shapes and decorations were all characteristic of the French factory.

In 1759 Louis XV dissolved the joint-stock company and bought all shares. He became sole owner of the *Manufacture Royale*. The factory buildings and the entire inventory—worth 760,950 louis—were entered as assets. Sèvres now had an art commission headed by Director Boileau, the chemist Hellot, Bachelier as head of the art department, and Falconet supervising the sculpture and modeling departments. In addition, there was a staff of numerous assistants, artists, and craftsmen. However, the experts in Sèvres were well aware that they were using merely an artificial substitute for true porcelain. Knowing this, Sèvres started early with experiments to reproduce Meissen's hard-paste porcelain.

In 1754 two "arcanists" appeared in Sèvres: their names were Busch and Stadelmayer, and they gave Boileau their promise that they would fire true porcelain. They wasted 12,000 louis and there was no success in sight. At that point Peter Anton Hannong began experiments that pointed in the right direction. In 1768 kaolin was discovered in St. Yrieix, and the chemist Macquer brought a sample to Paris. After 1769 Sèvres manufactured true porcelain. To distinguish it from the *Porcelaine de France,* it was called *Porcelaine Royale.*

Under Boileau's successor, Parent, the factory manufactured true porcelain almost exclusively. The results were debts in the amount of 247,000 louis. As a consequence Parent was imprisoned. In 1770 the factory employed 400 people. Orders arrived from all over Europe, and Catherine II of Russia greatly admired the lovely Sèvres porcelain. Her huge dinner service cost 300,000 louis and was the most expensive ever sold by Sèvres. Sèvres produced hard-paste and soft-paste porcelain simultaneously into the nineteenth century. The same holds true for its sculpture.

La Lanterne Magique (Fig. 77) was modeled after Boucher by Falconet in 1757. A great number of these biscuit figures are known, and the ones by Falconet are the most outstanding. (Lechevalier counted 623 biscuit figures and groups.) The first are modeled

Fig. 77. *"La Lanterne Magique."* Sèvres 1757. Model by Falconet

after Boucher by Blondeau and are called *Enfants de Boucher* (1753). Falconet's first figures are the *Enfants de la Rue* (children of the street) (1757), and then the *Lanterne Magique.* Falconet left Sèvres in 1766 and traveled to St. Petersburg, where he made the large bronze monument of Peter I.

With the death of Boileau in 1772 the time of splendor was over. Louis Simon Boizot, a man of talent who modeled large groups from hard porcelain, became the sculpture studio's new director, at a yearly salary of 40,000 louis. His assistant, La Riche, became superintendent of the modeling studio between 1780 and 1801. During this period works by famous contemporary artists were copied, notably those by Coypel, Oudry, Pigalle, Bouchardon, Clodion, Caffieri. Important personalities of the period were honored with portrait busts. The last years of the reign of Louis XVI were once again brilliant years for Sèvres. Even the Chinese Emperor Ch'ien Lung was presented with a diplomatic gift of Sèvres porcelain. Every aristocratic court ordered large table centerpieces from the French state factory, and they were executed in soft-paste or hard-paste porcelain according to the order. Louis XVI made Angivillier director of the entire enterprise and Johann Jakob Hettlinger from Winterthur became inspector.

Sèvres fortunes declined as a result of the establishment of new French factories. In spite of the prohibition from Sèvres they painted and gilded their porcelains. The French Revolution put an end to all luxuries. The factory was saved from complete destruction when the National Assembly decided in 1791 to make it common property of the citizens of France. Sèvres is in operation to this day.

The small French factories of Strassburg, Niderviller, Limoges, and Paris were hampered by the prohibitions imposed by Sèvres, even though these were loosened in the last years of the eighteenth century. This applied in particular to the Paris factories which were owned by the princely family. They were of no particular significance. Paul Hannong in Strassburg, together with some German technicians, produced his first hard-paste porcelain in 1753 from Passau kaolin. We have learned already that he was exiled from France two years later. However, in 1765 Joseph Hannong resumed production.

After 1735 a faience factory operated in Niderviller. With the help of workmen from Strassburg, a hard-paste porcelain factory was added in 1765. Very soon the kaolin from Passau was replaced by kaolin from St. Yrieix. As soon as Darnet had made his discovery, the owner of Niderviller bought a cartload of clay from St. Yrieix.

Limoges, situated in the vicinity of the kaolin deposit, also had a porcelain factory, which was founded by Massié and the brothers Grellet.

During the last years of the eighteenth century, porcelain factories in Paris proliferated, each one under the patronage of an aristocratic family. Around 1800 there were twenty-seven factories. The best known were those in the rue de Thiroux, rue de Bondy (Angoulême), la Roquette, Petit-Carrousel, Clignancourt, and Comte d'Artois. None of their products can compete with Sèvres.

ITALY

Venice

VEZZI

The first Italian porcelain was fired in 1720 in Venice, the *Republica di San Marco*. The goldsmith Francesco Vezzi, who with his brother Giuseppe had bought an aristocratic title for 100,000 ducats, was much admired as first factory owner. In 1719 he received permission to travel alone to Augsburg. At the time Augsburg was not only the most famous city for gold jewelry, but also a place familiar with the new porcelain invented by Meissen and manufactured even in Vienna. Meissen porcelain had been sent to Augsburg to be mounted in silver and gold. The arcanist was Hunger, who owed his knowledge to the kiln master Stoelzel in Vienna. It is not known where and how Vezzi met Hunger, but there is no doubt that Vezzi fired his first true porcelain with Hunger's help in 1720. He bought his clay in Aue, the same place from which Meissen too received its kaolin. Vezzi invested 30,000 ducats in his factory in San Nicolo. Carlo Ruzzini, later one of the Doges (rulers of Venice), was a shareholder in the new company and was responsible for the factory's ruin in 1727.

Fig. 78. Tea pot. Venice. Period of Vezzi, 1725

For seven years Vezzi produced remarkably fine porcelain. It compares well with Meissen's early period. His paste was extremely translucent and much purer than du Paquier's in Vienna.

Vezzi manufactured everything that was in demand by the Venetian society of his time—mainly dinner services, but also candelabras, large cooling vessels, and armorial plates. In his Venetian porcelain, the buyer's coat of arms was usually impressed in the paste or painted on the porcelain.

A typical example of Vezzi's craft in the period around 1725 is a tea pot (Fig. 78) decorated with paintings of comedians and popular characters. With its molded wreaths of acanthus leaves, it is vaguely reminiscent of Boettger's first porcelain pieces. The colors—iron-red, green, dark red, purple, blue, and some yellow—are well executed. With skill, Vezzi also developed the underglaze blue. It is assumed that all the workmen he employed were Italians, and we know the name of one painter and what he painted.

Fig. 79. Plate. San Giobbo around 1795. Painted by Cozzi

One plate is signed: *"Ludovico Ortolani nella fabrice di Porcellana in Venetia."*

The porcelain of Vezzi's first period is extremely rare today, not only because it is the only hard-paste porcelain of this early period, but also because very little porcelain was fired within the short span of seven years.

After the closing of Vezzi's factory the Senate issued a proclamation assuring support to anyone who wanted to open a faience or porcelain factory in Venice. It took thirty years, however, until the couple Hewelcke opened a new factory. We know little about it, but some of the tableware bears an incised *V* which is attributed to this factory.

COZZI

The third Italian factory—much more important than Vezzi—belonged to Geminiano Cozzi, who had gained experience with Hewelcke and was capable of producing his own porcelain. Cozzi built his first kilns in San Giobbo, and the Senate granted him a privilege one year later. He owed his initial success to some workmen who had run away from the factory in Nove, in particular the geologist Arduini, who showed Cozzi the white clay of Vicenza. During the first sixteen months Cozzi sold porcelain for 16,000 ducats, aided by the fact that the Senate had prohibited the import of foreign porcelain. The influx from France in 1793 and the occupation by Austria in 1812 put an end to the factory.

Cozzi utilized a raw material containing some kaolin. The chemist and director of Sèvres called it *"hybride de pâte-tendre."* Cozzi produced figures as well as tableware. The plate (Fig. 79) from one of his table services is painted with great care. The yellow-gray body is faultless, the pictorial decorations very good, but the glaze is dull. Cozzi also imitated the yellow backgrounds of Meissen. A few artists who worked with Cozzi are known: Ortolani, whose father had worked for Vezzi; two turners, Francesco Cecchetto and his son; Nerini; and the kiln master Costa. The modeler was Sebastian Lazzari.

Doccia

Doccia was the largest Italian porcelain factory, and it is still operating today. Its founder, Marchese Carlo Ginori of Florence, a dynamic personality, began in 1737 to examine the soil in the vicinity of Florence. He was not encouraged by the first firing. At that point, however, political events demanded that Senator Ginori travel to Vienna as head of a delegation to honor the new grand-duke of Tuscany, Francis III, husband of Maria Theresa. Ginori's eyes were wide open. He persuaded the Viennese porcelain painter Karl Wendelin Anreiter of Zirnfeld to come to Doccia. Although he was merely a painter, he knew something about the formula for the paste. Georg della Torre, paste mixer and kiln master with du Paquier, traveled with him. In 1738 the first clay arrived from the vicinity of Venice, and the kilns were constructed.

Among the first specialists was Gori for the kilns, the turner Mariotti, the Florentine painter Fiaschi, and the German painter Mohr. At the end of 1738, the most important positions were filled. Three years later Francis III granted them a privilege, and since 1746 Ginori has been selling porcelain all over the world.

The tableware was decorated by a technique called *a stampino*. Ornaments were cut out of vellum, then placed on the porcelain and stenciled in with blue color—a truly primitive procedure. In 1742 Ginori had thirty-seven employees, and fifteen years later there were as many as eighty. A coffee pot (Fig. 80) with a long neck and an elongated spout ending in a serpent's head is a typical example of that period. It is decorated with the coat of arms of Cardinal Stoppani, and the flower bouquets on each side are reminiscent of the German flowers of Meissen or du Paquier. Anreiter had returned to Vienna by the time this coffee pot was painted in 1755. Also manufactured were strange double-walled vessels, the outer wall perforated, which remind one of the small *blanc de chine* ewers of Fukien.

Through the years Doccia improved its paste, and after 1770 Lorenzo, who managed the factory after his father's death in 1757, used a tin glaze which lent a lighter appearance to the tableware. He worked

Fig. 80. Coffee Pot. Doccia 1755. Painted for Cardinal Stoppani

with much success, adding new artists to his staff and enriching the variety of Doccia's models considerably. The use of rococo forms, which had been introduced by Carlo, was continued by his son until 1791. Doccia's most famous decorations are the *a galloto* and the *a tulipano*. One of the services is decorated with a red and gold rooster, the other with a stylized tulip, again in red and gold with green leaves. After the Napoleonic invasion a pure white paste was used in Doccia, perhaps of clay from St. Yrieix.

Doccia also carried a large stock of figures. The well-known Casparo Bruschi was the modeler. He worked in Doccia from 1737 to 1780 and created an immense variety of both small and very large groups. With the latter he hoped to compete with Kaendler in Meissen. Massimiliano Soldani-Benzi was another modeler, and his wax models are preserved in the factory's museum. One particular decor, up to now attributed to the factory in Naples, was introduced in Doccia almost from the beginning. These are relief decorations frequently depicting scenes from the *Metamorphoses* of Ovid and applied to the walls of jars.

Doccia's themes were wide-ranging, from biblical scenes and street criers to the by-now familiar comedians (who, after all, were at home in Italy). There was nothing that Doccia did not offer for sale.

Capo di Monte

The former director of the ceramic department of London's Victoria and Albert Museum called Capo di Monte the most important of the Italian factories of the eighteenth century. It is astonishing how much this factory accomplished during the short period from 1743 to 1759. Charles of Bourbon, the son of Philip V of Spain, became King of Naples and Sicily through his second marriage, to Elisabeth Farnese. His third wife, Maria Amalia Christina, daughter of August II, King of Poland and Elector of Saxony, brought him seventeen porcelain services from the Meissen factory as a marriage gift in 1738. Charles was an able monarch and his name, linked to the excavations of Herculaneum, has survived through posterity. He was so delighted with his wife's porcelain that he was seized with the porcelain mania. Near his newly built castle in Capo di Monte, diligent experiments were conducted to produce the new paste. In 1743 the King founded his porcelain factory in Naples. The paste was a fine white *pâte tendre* as in France.

The paste mixer was a mine expert, Livio Scheppers, but because of his dishonesty he was soon replaced by his son Gaetano. Giuseppe Gricci was superintendent of the modelers, and the painters worked under Giovanni Caselli. Johann Sigismund Fischer of Meissen painted in Capo di Monte after 1754 but died of mushroom poisoning four years later. He was succeeded by Luigi Restile. The paintings of Capo di Monte are exquisite. Giuseppe della Torre specialized in battle scenes, seascapes, and landscapes. Maria Caselli painted flowers and was also noted for her chinoiseries. The technical expertise appears to have been well advanced. It was possible to furnish the Portici Room as a porcelain chamber similar to the one in Vienna. Sculptures of Chinese figures in various positions were attached to the walls and ceiling.

The first objects produced by the factory were shell-shaped snuff boxes, cane handles, tea sets, tureens, ceramic flowers like those of Vincennes. The specialist for these flowers was Gaetano Fumo.

Capo di Monte modeled numerous figures. The old *Commedia dell'Arte* figures were much in demand and were modeled by Gricci. The four Pantaloons playing their musical instruments while sitting on a rocky mound (Fig. 81) were created by this artist. Somewhat ghostlike with their black-brown masks and purple kerchiefs, they are one of Capo di Monte's largest groups. Gricci's artistic rank is equal to Kaendler's of Meissen. His street vendors, young lovers, men and women servants, and allegorical presentations of the seasons belong to the most outstanding works of art ever created in porcelain.

After the death of Ferdinand III, Charles II of Naples became King of Spain. He had become so attached to his porcelain factory that he moved it to Spain. In October 1759 three ships set out from Naples in the direction of Alicante. On board were forty-four workmen with their families and eighty-eight tons of material and supplies. The factory was rebuilt outside Madrid in Buon Retiro. Gaetano Scheppers, his son Carlos, and Giuseppe Ricci had come along.

Fig. 81. Group with four Pantaloons. Capo di Monte around 1750. Model by G. Gricci

The porcelain of Buon Retiro is difficult to distinguish from Capo di Monte's, especially the porcelain of the early period, since the raw materials still came from Naples. As in Naples, porcelain cabinets were built in Madrid and Aranjuez. When Charles died in 1788, the inventory was offered for sale but little was bought. Until 1794 the factory was in inexperienced hands and worked without much success.

Venice, Doccia, and Capo di Monte were the most important Italian factories of the eighteenth century. There were other, smaller factories, such as Vinovo near Turin, where Johann Viktor Brodel manufactured hard-paste porcelain for a short period together with Peter Hannong from Strassburg. In 1752 Pasquale Antonibon began experiments with the production of porcelain in Nove near Bassano. He sold his first cups in Venice. His kiln was built by Sigismund Fischer in 1752 in order to fire porcelain *ad uso Sassonia*. There were small porcelain factories in Este and Treviso. A second factory in Naples, erected by the son of Ferdinand IV in 1771, never produced anything of great importance.

ENGLAND

English porcelain seldom displayed an original style of its own, but usually could be traced back to German, French, Chinese, and Japanese porcelains (Dixon). England used four different types of porcelain paste. One of these, used in Chelsea, Derby, and Longton Hall, was a glass-like frit of chalk and white clay. A similar paste, but with the addition of bone paste, was used in Bow and Lowestoft. Worcester, Caughley, and Liverpool used a soap paste to which was added steatit (magnesium silicate) instead of clay. A hard porcelain paste containing kaolin was used in Plymouth, Bristol, and Newhall.

It is impossible to discuss here the many large and small factories, but I have chosen the most important ones—Chelsea, Derby, Bow, and Bristol—and will illustrate one example of each.

Chelsea

Chelsea, the oldest English factory, is mentioned for the first time in 1747, when a London paper, the *Trademan,* offered pitchers in the shape of "Goat and Bee." They bear as a mark an incised triangle with the name Chelsea. Some of these vessels are dated 1747. The first owner of England's first factory was Charles Gouyn, but he sold it as early as 1750 to Nicolas Sprimont, a goldsmith from the Netherlands who brought great fame to the factory. He sold it in 1769 to James Cox, who passed it on to William Duesbury of Derby after only one year. Duesbury managed the factory until 1784. His products are known today as Chelsea-Derby. In 1784 the Chelsea factory, including kilns, workshops, and molds, was destroyed. A few molds were saved and taken to Derby.

Chelsea porcelain can be dated by its marks and falls into four distinct periods:

An incised triangle (the triangle period), 1745–1749
An incised anchor, 1750–1755
A painted red anchor, 1756–1758
A golden anchor, 1758–1770.

All periods had one trait in common. They imitated Meissen's tableware, its painting, and the sculpture of its figures. Chelsea is the typical imitator of Meissen's early period. The figures which derived their style from the "Girl in a Swing" were an English novelty. Otherwise, although their molds were formed after the pattern book of George Edwards, we find the typical Meissen plate designs, with their borders, river landscapes, German flowers, and Korean birds, exactly as Kaendler had modeled them!

The second period, like the first, was characterized by Meissen forms. The tableware, painted by J. H. O'Neale with fabled animals, is typical of that period. Barlow's illustrated edition of *Aesop's Fables* (1687) was used as a model. The period of the red anchor was the great period of English porcelain. By then, the turners, formers, modelers, and painters had acquired enough experience. The figures of that period are among the best that English porcelain has to offer.

Chelsea's most charming specialty was its "toys," small scent bottles for handbags in the shapes of figures (Fig. 82) Some have inscriptions such as *"Le Vin aide l'Amour"* (wine helps love), *"Fleuve d'Amour"* (love potion), *"Je suis votre Captive"* (I am your prisoner), *"Heure du Berger Fidèle"* (the hour of the faithful shepherd), etc.

Fig. 82. "Chelsea Toys." Chelsea 1756–1758

The era of the golden anchor brought an entirely new style, more elegant but less genuine. The most fanciful rococo shapes were resurrected. Vases were made with divided handles, and backgrounds were colored, particularly in blue. After the Seven Years' War had done much damage to Meissen, Sèvres moved into the foreground. Even *rose Pompadour* now found its faithful imitators.

Derby

In his workshop in London, between 1752 and 1753, William Duesbury painted porcelain figures for the factories in Chelsea, Bow, Derby, and Staffordshire. In his workbook we find entries on figures from "Darby." It is thought that they were made by one André Planché in Derby between 1750 and 1755. He received support from the co-owner of the Cockpit Hill faience factory and the banker John Heath.

The premises became too small in 1756 and a new factory was built on the Nottingham Road. As soon as Planché had mastered the mysteries of the clay mixtures, he disappeared. In 1770 Duesbury bought the ailing Chelsea factory and added it to Derby. When Heath went bankrupt in 1779, Duesbury became the sole owner. His son succeeded him after his death in 1786 and went into partnership with

Fig. 83. "The Pig." Derby 1770

the miniature-painter Kean from Paris. Kean sold the factory in 1811 but it remained in existence until 1848. Derby manufactured everything that could be made out of porcelain. Among its earliest figures are Chinese and allegorical figures, Neptune, Jupiter and the Eagle, Venus and Cupid.

One satirical group from the period around 1770 is called "The Pig" (Fig. 83). Instead of offering her church tax in the form of a pig, as was the custom during the sixteenth century, the peasant woman offers her newborn to the priest.

The son of Johann Jakob Spengler, director of Zurich's porcelain factory, was one of Derby's workmen in 1780. A few groups have artistic value: the Russian Shepherd, the Blind Beggar and His Daughter, among others. They were modeled by Spengler.

Bow

In 1774 two merchants, Edward Heylin and Thomas Frye from Stratford-le-Bow in the east end of London, requested a patent for "a certain material" which was supposed to have superior qualities to the porcelain imported from abroad. Four years

Fig. 84. Harlequin. Bow around 1755

later Frye received a new patent because he had added ashes from animal bones to his paste. In 1750 the factory became the property of the two merchants Weatherby and Crowther. Frye remained as manager until 1759. The lovely forms of the tableware and the artistic figures were due to Thomas Frye, and the factory fell into a rapid decline after his departure. Weatherby died in 1762, and his partner went bankrupt a year later. That same year the factory was bought by William Duesbury, but he closed it soon after. Bow's first tableware is decorated with Japanese designs and the painters later copied the French flowers of Mennecy and Meissen's early designs.

Some Bow figures are marked with a *T* or a *Te*. They were modeled by the elusive modeler Tebo, who also worked in Bristol and Worcester, and, until he fell into disgrace there, at the Wedgwood factory in Etruria. The Harlequin (Fig. 84) shown here is an unmistakable Kaendler model that Bow stole from Meissen. The purple, yellow, and blue colors are typical of Bow. The blossoms at the base stand out against a poison green.

Bristol

Bristol serves as an illustration of one of the small English factories. William Cookworthy, the Quaker chemist from Plymouth, received a patent for the manufacture of true porcelain in 1758. He based his experiments on letters from the Jesuit priest Father d'Entrecolles in China, who described how Chinese porcelain was made. After a long search he found suitable porcelain clay in Cornwall. With Richard Champion as partner, he opened his factory first in Plymouth but moved it to Bristol after two years. In 1773 Champion bought out Cookworthy and became sole owner of the Bristol factory. After eight years he was ruined financially and sold his arcanum to the Newhall factory to then make hard-paste porcelain.

The tableware and figures are poorly decorated and have no special artistic value, but they represent the first Meissen English hard-paste porcelain.

The figures are exact copies of Longton Hall, because Cookworthy had bought that factory's molds in 1760. Among the few figures is "The Seasons" (Fig. 85). The girl symbolizing spring is part of this series. It should be dated around 1775. Bristol had no mark of its own.

Fig. 85. "The Seasons." Bristol around 1775

DENMARK

Copenhagen

The origin of the Copenhagen factory goes back to 1760. It was the ambition of King Frederick V to have a factory in his own country. The first experiments, which were not successful, were conducted by Johann Jakob Mehlhorn, son of Johann Georg Mehlhorn, the Meissen underglaze-blue painter and glass cutter. When Louis Fournier was called from Chantilly, Copenhagen began to manufacture soft-paste porcelain in small quantities until 1766. Only twenty pieces from that period are known today.

In 1766 the King died and was succeeded by his son, the seventeen-year-old Christian VII. There was much hope among the people that he would make a clean sweep of the prevalent corruption, but these hopes proved to be in vain. The winter of 1766–1767 brought much hunger, misery, and rising prices. Nevertheless, the court indulged in luxuries and amusements, and the mounting anger of the population against their young monarch was justified. It was out of the question to keep the factory in operation. In the meantime, the apothecary and chemist Franz Heinrich Mueller had done his own research. In 1773 he was able to show his first pieces of translucent hard-paste porcelain to the King. However, the situation in the state of Denmark was not conducive to the establishment of a porcelain factory.

Only two years later, under the reign of the Queen Mother Juliana Maria, was it feasible to make plans for Mueller's factory. A joint-stock company was founded. Mueller himself had a share in it and was appointed director. J. Ch. Bayer was chief painter, Anton Carl Luplau from Fuerstenberg was master modeler. In spite of the most stringent economies, the debts grew to such an extent that the court was compelled to take over the factory. The first salesrooms were opened in 1780, but the political situation hindered progress repeatedly. In 1784 Crown Prince Frederick deposed his feeble-minded father and Juliana Maria. The import of foreign porcelain was then forbidden.

The most famous service ever made in Copenhagen was the *"Flora Danica"* (Fig. 86) for Empress Catherine II of Russia. It was painted by Bayer and took twelve years to complete. One thousand three hundred thirty-five pieces were finished in 1790. In spite of the Empress's death, work on the service continued. It was planned for one hundred persons—the breakfast service alone consisted of 632 pieces—and had been ordered by Crown Prince Frederick. The famous botanist Theodor Holmakjord, a pupil of Linné, designed the decoration, which features plants whose names are inscribed at the base of the individual dishes. The plate illustrated here is named "Scabiosa columbaria." The large service was completed in 1805.

Although the tableware predominated, Copenhagen also produced figures. They were typical of the turn of the century: family groups, popular characters, a Peasant Girl Holding a Hen, a Cow Being Milked, a Flute Player, groups of children. The use of these ordinary folk as models for Copenhagen's sculpture represented a radical change from the elegant motifs of the baroque and rococo periods. The factory is still in operation today.

Fig. 86. Plate from the *"Flora Danica"* service for the Empress Catherine II. Copenhagen 1790

HOLLAND

Oude Loosdrecht

A hard-paste porcelain factory under the direction of Count Gronsfeld-Dieppenbrock was founded in Weesp in 1759. The kaolin came from Germany; Niklaus Paul was its first arcanist. The rare Weesp porcelain, pure white in color, exhibited forms and designs copied from the German factories. A few figures were modeled by Nicolas Gauron of Tournai. After Weesp was closed in 1771 because business was poor, Pastor Johannes de Mol, who had experimented with porcelain in Oude Loosdrecht, hired the artists and took over some of the molds. But only with the help of Victor Louis Gerverot and some clay from Passau did he succeed in producing true porcelain in 1774. At the pastor's advice, Gerverot and some workmen were sent to get experience at Schrezheim, a factory that had ceased production. They were permitted to use the kilns, the paste, and the molds.

The first salesroom was opened in Amsterdam and sold merchandise from Weesp, Schrezheim, and Loosdrecht. In 1778 sixty adults and twenty-five children worked in Mol's factory, among them seven foreigners. Unfortunately we don't know any names aside from Gerverot's.

The importation of inexpensive English stoneware proved a catastrophe for the expensive Dutch porcelain. Mol had to take out a loan of 130,000 florins in 1779 and another of 200,000 florins in 1780. But it was impossible to prevent bankruptcy in the years that followed. The collapse came in 1782. It is quite likely that business worries were responsible for Mol's death in November of the same year.

Mol offered beautiful designs with excellent decorations. A small dish showing a chemist in his laboratory (Fig. 87) is exquisitely painted. It may be dated around 1775. The painter is not known, but it may be the work of Cornelius Buys, who is supposed to have painted for the factory. After Mol's death, the creditors decided to move the factory to Amstel, where until 1814 it manufactured porcelain in the style of Loosdrecht.

The Hague

The porcelain of The Hague comes from three different sources. After 1775 the German merchant Anton Lyncker, together with Johann Lyncker, conducted a brisk trade with German porcelain. He could save the considerable expense of customs duties by importing unpainted porcelain and painting it himself. This he did until 1778 when he decided to open his own factory. He bought the kaolin in Germany. Friedrich Bevering of Kiel, Anton Kissinger of Mainz, Johann Philipp Miller and Johann Nerwein of Frankenthal worked as painters with him. They decorated tableware with flowers, landscapes, birds, genre scenes, and ornaments. Christof Killer of Mainz was the former. The paintings of The Hague were veritable masterpieces, and they were so famous that they were sold to such distant places as Turkey.

There were forty workmen in Lyncker's factory until 1781, the year of his death. His widow kept the factory in operation until 1784, when the son, Johann Lyncker, took over. Married to an aristocratic

Fig. 87. Platter. Oude Loosdrecht around 1775. Probably painted by Cornelius Buys

nun who had escaped from her monastery, Johann liked to live in noble style and had lost money because of legal difficulties. He was a swindler and not at all diligent as factory manager, and the factory was closed due to bankruptcy in 1790.

Three types of porcelain were decorated in The Hague: porcelain produced in its own factory; imported white porcelain from Ansbach, Volkstedt, and Meissen; and *pâte tendre* from Tournai, the Belgian factory. The small tureen with saucer (Fig. 88) depicted here is made of soft-paste porcelain from Tournai and beautifully decorated with flowers and landscapes. Lyncker painted the borders with their alternating blue background and purple wreaths in an extremely tasteful manner, and the design was no doubt his own.

Fig. 88. "*Confiturie*" with saucer. Porcelain from Tournai. The Hague around 1780

BELGIUM

Tournai

One of the most important factories producing soft-paste porcelain was Tournai. J. F. Peterinck converted it from a faience factory with assistance from the state. It was given the title *"Manufacture Imperiale Royale,"* because the privilege had been granted by the Empress Maria Theresa and her son-in-law, Prince Charles Alexander of Lothringen. Robert Dubois, whom we have met previously in Sèvres and Chantilly, was its director and arcanist. He brought the secret of soft-paste porcelain from Sèvres to Tournai. Peterinck managed his factory for forty-five years, until three years before his death in 1799 at the age of eighty. In 1800 his son built a stoneware factory and the old porcelain factory gradually fell into decay.

Fig. 89. Plate with green chinoiseries. Tournai. *Pâte tendre*. Around 1770

Tournai produced tableware, figures, and groups. The illustrated tableware with green chinoiserie (Fig. 89) is one of the rarest of its kind. It was produced in the 1760s. The plate may have been painted by Henri Josef Duvivier, who had come from England and was superintendent of the painting department. It was his responsibility to train the apprentice painters. In 1775 we also find among the painters the name of Georg Christoph Lindenmann, who had painted in various German factories.

Copenhagen produced the large *"Flora Danica"* service, but Tournai too had its historic service consisting of 950 individual pieces, decorated with birds after the work of Buffon. Tournai's groups are elegant and well-finished artistically: amorous groups in the style of Chelsea, a large Pietà, a work of Gauron. As modelers, besides Nicolas Gauron, the names Lecreux, Antoine Gillis, and Josef Willems are known. Gauron had previously worked in Mennecy, Vincennes, and Chelsea, which explains the similarity between the Tournai figures and those from France and England. As the groups are not marked, it is not easy to recognize them. The fine paste and delicate painting may serve as guideposts.

MARKS OF THE FACTORIES DISCUSSED IN THIS BOOK

Meissen, 1723–1724
Meissen Royal Factory
Meissen Royal Porcelain Factory

Meissen AR (Augustus Rex)
(Only pieces belonging to the King)

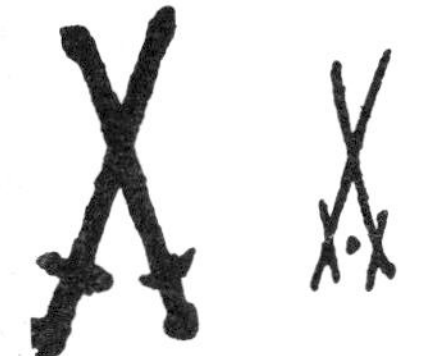

Meissen
Swords, 1725 to
present day
Point period, 1763–1774
Marcolini period, 1774–1813

Vienna
Du Paquier, no mark
Imperial Factory, 1744–1864

Hoechst
1750–1796

Berlin
Wegeli, 1752–1757
Gotzkowski, 1761–1763
State Factory, 1763 to present day

Fuerstenberg, 1753 to present day

Frankenthal
Hannong, 1755–1762
Karl Theodor, 1762–1800

Ludwigsburg, 1758–1796

Nymphenburg, 1755 to present day

Ansbach, 1758–1785
all marks simultaneously

Kelsterbach, 1761–1790

Fulda, 1765–1790
Kreuz, 1765–1780
Factory of the Prince, 1780–1788

Kassel, 1766–1788
both marks simultaneously

Wuerzburg, 1775–1780
both simultaneously
Caspar Geiger, Wuerzburg

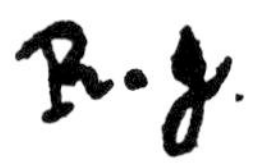

Gotha, 1757–1805
Rotberg

Volkstedt,
1767 to present day

Closter-Veilsdorf,
1761 to present day

Wallendorf,
1764 to present day

Limbach, 1772–1788

Zurich, 1763–1790

Nyon, 1781–1813

St. Cloud, 1693–1766
St. Cloud Trou
both marks simultaneously

Chantilly, 1725–1800

.D.V.

Mennecy, 1748–1773

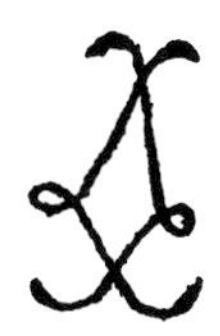

Vincennes-Sèvres,
1738 to present day

Venice
Vezzi, 1720–1727?

Cozzi, 1764–1812

Doccia, late 18th century

Naples
Capo di Monte, 1743–1759

Naples, after 1771

Chelsea,
1745–1750 and 1750–1769

Derby, 1770–1780

Bow, 1750–1760

Copenhagen
Fournier Period, 1759–1769
State Factory, 1773 to present day

Oude Loosdrecht, 1771–1784

The Hague, 1773–1790

Tournai, 1751, earliest mark

INDEX

Italicized numbers refer to illustrations.